AMERICA'S HEROES

Inspiring Stories of Courage, Sacrifice and Patriotism

SP
L.L.C.

AMERICA'S HEROES

Inspiring Stories of Courage, Sacrifice and Patriotism

Publisher: **Peter L. Bannon**
Senior Managing Editors: **Joseph J. Bannon Jr.** and **Susan M. Moyer**
Art Director: **K. Jeffrey Higgerson**

Graphic Designer: **Kenneth J. O'Brien**
Imaging: **Christina Cary**
Photo Research Editor: **Erin M. Linden-Levy**

ISBN 1-58261-468-7

"Often you see generations

of firefighters. There's a

sense of responsibility to

the public that is learned.

… It can be said they never

had a choice. Being a hero is

just in their blood."

CONTENTS

DEDICATION

There is no simple answer to the question of what drives someone to be a hero. Experts speculate that people spurred to heroism do so because they have a profound respect for human life. Or because they have a strong sense of empathy and self-esteem. Moral courage and physical strength also appear as important contributors to the trait of heroism. There may even be a biological component: some people simply have it in their blood to be heroes.

What does seem clear, though, is that the trait of heroism lives somewhere inside all of us. Hopefully, we never have to face a moment that requires us to act heroically. But as the events of September 11, 2001, showed the world, when that moment arrives, America's heroes respond without hesitation.

We proudly dedicate this book to the untold number of heroes whose stories rise high above the cowardice of the terrorist attacks on the World Trade Center and the Pentagon. Firefighters, police officers, building workers, medical personnel, civilian volunteers and many more worked tirelessly in hopes of saving just one more life. We celebrate these incredible stories of heroism.

Our sadness, however, is that all of the stories will never be told. Many of the heroes of that terrible day perished in the wreckage, and their stories of heroism were forever lost with them. So we honor all the heroes—and the people they saved and those they tried to save—by recounting many of these brave acts of September 11, 2001, and the aftermath.

Through the inspiring stories and emotional images in this book, we can remember with great pride the way that all of America stood together in the face of unspeakable horror.

In some ways, this renewed spirit of national unity may serve as a template for our own everyday lives. Whether it's helping a neighbor, comforting a friend or simply hugging a family member, we may have a new appreciation for these otherwise ordinary acts. And that, in the end, may be the greatest legacy of America's heroes.

Constructing the Heart
of the New York Skyline

When they debuted at the official ribbon-cutting ceremony in 1973, the two glistening 110-story towers of New York City's World Trade Center were 1,362 and 1,368 feet high—more than 100 feet taller than the city's other world height record holder—the Empire State Building. The towers held the height record only briefly, however. Even as they neared completion, work had begun on Chicago's Sears Tower, which would reach 1,450 feet.

Minoru Yamasaki was selected over a dozen other architects and was presented with an explicit design proposal: 12 million square feet of floor area on a 16-acre site, which also had to accommodate new facilities for the Hudson tubes and subway connections—all with a budget under $500 million for the two towers. After studying more than 100 schemes in model form, Yamasaki decided on a two-tower development. One tower became unreasonable in size and was structurally infeasible, while several towers would look "too much like a housing project." Two towers could provide reasonable office space on each floor

(43,200 square feet), take advantage of the magnificent views and allow for a manageable structural system.

Before foundation excavation began, the 500 x 1,000-foot site was enclosed by a three-foot-thick, 70-foot-high concrete cutoff wall and keyed three feet into rock. Excavation was complicated by two nearby subway tubes that had to be supported without service interruption. A six-level basement was built in the foundation hole. Groundbreaking for the construction took place on August 5, 1966, and steel construction began in August 1968. The excavation and sale of 1.2 million cubic yards of earth and rock created $90 million of revenue for the project owner, the Port of New York Authority. Instead of being trucked off for disposal, soil was used to create 23 acres of fill in the Hudson River adjacent to the WTC site. It has since been developed as Battery Park City.

The twin towers had the world's highest load-bearing walls. They were designed as vertical cantilevered steel tubes. Adjacent city streets were

"The World Trade Center should, because of its importance, become a living representation of man's belief in humanity, his need for individual dignity, his belief in the cooperation of men, and through this cooperation his ability to find greatness."

narrow, congested and offered little storage space. Each of the 200,000 pieces of steel used in the construction had to arrive at the right place at the right time—and for the most part, they did. One of the industry's earliest computer-programmed control systems, which took engineers six months to set up, helped accomplish this.

The first tenant occupancy of One WTC was in December 1970, while occupancy of Two WTC began in January of 1972. The opening ceremony for the WTC took place on April 4, 1973.

The World Trade Center site comprised 16 acres, with seven buildings grouped around a five-acre central plaza. The north and south towers were the huge monoliths recognizable as the heart of the New York City skyline. They could be seen from as far away as the northern part of the Bronx, the easternmost part of Queens and from certain points in lower Brooklyn. From the observation decks at the top of the towers, it was possible to see 45 miles in every direction.

"The World Trade Center should," said Yamasaki, "because of its importance, become a living representation of man's belief in humanity, his need for individual dignity, his belief in the cooperation of men, and through this cooperation his ability to find greatness."

Key Facts about the World Trade Center

SIZE:	Seven buildings, including the twin 110-floor towers. The others: a 47-story office building, two nine-story office buildings, an eight-story U.S. Customs office and a 22-story hotel.
HEIGHT:	The twin towers were 1,362 and 1,368 feet tall.
COST:	Roughly $1.25 billion for the seven buildings.
RENTABLE SPACE:	12 million square feet of rentable office space; some 1,200 companies and organizations leased space.
WORKERS:	Roughly 50,000 people were employed in the twin towers.
TOURISTS:	On average, 90,000 tourists and business visitors each day.
CHIEF ARCHITECT:	Minoru Yamasaki.

Excerpts from President Bush's Address to the Nation on September 11, 2001

Today, our fellow citizens, our way of life, our very freedom came under attack in a series of deliberate and deadly terrorist acts. The victims were in airplanes or in their offices; secretaries, business men and women, military and federal workers, moms and dads, friends and neighbors.

These acts of mass murder were intended to frighten our nation into chaos and retreat. But they have failed. Our country is strong. A great people has been moved to defend a great nation. Terrorist attacks can shake the foundations of our biggest buildings, but they cannot touch the foundation of America. These acts shatter steel, but they cannot dent the steel of American resolve.

Today, our nation saw evil, the very worst of human nature, and we responded with the best of America, with the daring of our rescue workers, with the caring for strangers and neighbors who came to give blood and help in any way they could.

The functions of our government continue without interruption. Federal agencies in Washington which had to be evacuated today are reopen for essential personnel tonight and will be open for business tomorrow.

Our financial institutions remain strong, and the American economy will be open for business as well.

I've directed the full resources of our intelligence and law enforcement communities to find those responsible and bring them to justice. We will make no distinction between the terrorists who committed these acts and those who harbor them.

This is a day when all Americans from every walk of life unite in our resolve for justice and peace. America has stood down enemies before, and we will do so this time.

None of us will ever forget this day, yet we go forward to defend freedom and all that is good and just in our world.

Thank you. Good night and God bless America.

"*This is a day when all Americans from every walk of life unite in our resolve for justice and peace.*"

Timeline of the Terrorist Attacks

7:59 a.m.   American Flight 11 with 92 people leaves Boston's Logan Airport for Los Angeles.

8:01 a.m.   United Flight 93 with 45 people leaves Newark Airport for San Francisco.

8:10 a.m.   American Flight 77 with 64 people leaves Washington's Dulles Airport for Los Angeles.

8:14 a.m.   United Flight 175 with 65 people leaves Boston for Los Angeles.

8:48 a.m.   American Flight 11 crashes into north tower of World Trade Center.

9:06 a.m.   United Flight 175 crashes into south tower of World Trade Center.

9:17 a.m.   Federal Aviation Administration shuts down all New York City-area airports.

9:21 a.m.   All bridges and tunnels into Manhattan closed.

9:31 a.m.   In Sarasota, Fla., President Bush calls the crashes an "apparent terrorist attack on our country."

9:43 a.m.   American Flight 77 crashes into Pentagon.

9:48 a.m.   U.S. Capitol and White House's West Wing evacuated.

9:49 a.m.   FAA bars all aircraft takeoffs across United States.

9:55 a.m.   South tower of World Trade Center collapses.

10:10 a.m.   United Flight 93 crashes in Pennsylvania field.

10:29 a.m.   North tower of World Trade Center collapses.

11 a.m.   New York mayor orders evacuation of lower Manhattan.

1:04 p.m.   From Barksdale Air Force base in Louisiana, Bush announces U.S. military on high alert worldwide.

2:51 p.m.   Navy dispatches missile destroyers to New York, Washington.

3:07 p.m.   Bush arrives at U.S. Strategic Command at Offutt Air Force Base in Nebraska.

5:25 p.m.   Empty 47-story Seven World Trade Center collapses.

7 p.m.   Bush arrives at White House.

8:30 p.m.   Bush addresses the nation and vows to "find those responsible and bring them to justice."

"The time has come for us to re-establish the rights for which we stand—to re-assert our inalienable rights to human dignity, self-respect, self-reliance—to be again the kind of people who once made America great."

—J. Ollie Edmunds, poet

Hundreds Deployed
for Attack Rescue

By Sharon Theimer

WASHINGTON (AP)—After the first of four planes crashed in three U.S. cities in a morning of chaos and terror, federal emergency officials acted according to plan.

The Federal Emergency Management Agency carried out President Bush's orders to implement a national emergency response plan after the first of two planes struck the World Trade Center in New York.

By afternoon, hundreds of rescue workers were sent to search for survivors and recover remains. Meanwhile, Bush, Vice President Dick Cheney and congressional leaders were moved to secure locations.

Transportation Secretary Norman Mineta ordered commercial air traffic grounded until at least Wednesday afternoon.

"These terrorist acts are designed to steal the confidence of Americans," Mineta said. "We will restore that confidence."

FEMA notified government agencies to react to the highest-level emergency, a "level one" like those declared after the 1989 Loma Prieta earthquake in California, the 1995 Oklahoma City bombing, hurricanes and severe flooding.

FEMA and roughly two dozen other federal and volunteer agencies will back up the states involved however necessary, including search and rescue, transportation, medical and mortuary support, said Steven Presgraves, FEMA's emergency teams unit leader.

The agencies also evaluate damage, cope with hazardous materials and provide food, water, shelter and electricity.

At least eight urban search-and-rescue task forces were dispatched to New York City, which Bush declared a disaster area, and four to the Pentagon. That building, the world's largest office building, was hit by a plane within an hour of the Trade Center crashes.

"They can locate, identify and rescue people in confined spaces," Presgraves said. "Recovery of victims, finding remains is also very important to family members. To do that safely, these search-and-rescue teams have the ability to shore up weak buildings."

Rescuers take a few moments for lunch at one of many stations set up to feed and comfort the workers.

"These terrorist acts are designed to steal the confidence of Americans. We will restore that confidence."

The searchers include teams from Massachusetts, Ohio, Missouri, Pennsylvania, Indiana, California, Virginia, Maryland and Tennessee. A search was also underway for victims of a fourth crash in rural Pennsylvania.

The emergency plan was developed in the late 1980s and was improved after the 1995 Oklahoma City bombing, Presgraves said. After that attack, FEMA learned to stage resources to avoid bottlenecks rather than bring everything in at once, he said. "We talk about right resource, right time, right place," Presgraves said.

"We will be here for as long as it takes."

"We talk about right resource, right time, right place."

AMERICA'S HEROES

"I had never really thought about the name 'United States' before, but 'United' now has a very powerful meaning. I couldn't be more proud to be an American."

—Lt. Col. Patty Horoho

Cave Explorer
Rushed to Ground Zero

By J.M. Hirsch

CONCORD, N.H. (AP)—By the time a second airliner slammed into the World Trade Center, Russell Keat knew his mind was urgently needed.

There would be rubble and wreckage. There would be bodies as twisted and broken as the debris that buried them.

Somebody would need to crawl through it, finding and mapping safe paths for other rescuers to follow. And that is Keat's specialty.

Keat, 40, is a rarity when it comes to search and rescue missions, of which he has participated in hundreds, from airliner crashes to collapsed buildings to people trapped in caves.

He is trained to work underground, to map the crevices, tunnels and holes in the debris that could fall several stories. He makes the search for survivors possible.

"In some ways my whole life was leading up to this," he said in a telephone interview from his Grantham home.

After the attacks, Keat didn't wait for a call. He grabbed his gear, stopped by the elementary school to say goodbye to his 5- and 6-year-old daughters, then headed for New York.

Though his mission was mapping, Keat went in with 350 pounds of gear, including enough food and water for him to stay with a trapped survivor for up to a week, if necessary.

"We're looking for human life, we're looking to support and evacuate. Or if they're trapped, to stay there with them. Once we can make a life sign that's trapped, we never leave."

Keat didn't find anyone alive, though he found plenty of remnants of lives.

"You'll pick up a picture that somebody obviously had in their office of their kids or a loved one," he said. "In some ways one of the hugest feelings is a sense of reverence. You are walking in the personal spaces of people, and even as you're wriggling through stuff that is awful, this is still their space."

It was his love of exploring caves that got Keat interested in underground rescue missions.

"In some ways my whole
life was leading up to this."

He often works with Shenandoah Mountain Rescue and says his training began even earlier.

"My father was actually an architect with experience in steel in large buildings, so a lot of what I was using was learned as a kid crawling through the guts of buildings as they were being built."

As part of Keat's mapping task, he watches for signs of trouble, including possible hazardous chemicals that could leak from businesses, such as medical offices.

That information is recorded, at the scene in spray-painted messages on the rubble, and on maps sent back to those organizing the rescue attempts.

By the time Keat and his team finished mapping the pile, he had endured some close calls, from dangerous precipices to clouds of noxious asbestos dust. He was treated four times for smoke inhalation.

"The worst moment was when we were probing the voids," he said. "I was going pretty much near vertical. I got to the bottom of it and there's this buckled over piece of concrete. I was looking straight down into eight stories of empty."

But there also were bright moments, as when a member of his team found an American flag. When the team came out of the rubble, Keat's teammate hung the flag on the tower's now fallen antenna.

"For five seconds there while he planted the flag, he was leading the world," Keat said.

"Once we can make a life sign that's trapped, we never leave."

People Help Each Other Amid Chaos

By Christopher Sullivan

Even as they scrambled to flee World Trade Center offices, workers paused to count heads, making sure their deskmates were there. Construction workers cobbled together stretchers from materials at their Manhattan worksite. On the House floor, members of Congress hugged and sang "God Bless America."

In the midst of the chaos, humanity emerged from Tuesday's terrorist attacks.

At the Hilton Hotel at Boston's Logan Airport, where clergymen rushed to be with relatives of passengers on two airliners that crashed into the World Trade Center, the Rev. David Keene said much the same. "Mostly we listen and hug," he added.

Jason Beerman rushed toward the twin towers complex as soon as he heard news of the attacks. But how could he find his older brother, Kenton, in the mayhem? Somehow, he did. As 24-year-old Kenton emerged into daylight from the gloom of a stairwell, one of the first faces he saw was Jason's.

"I don't know how he found me," Kenton said. "He just hugged me and said, 'I'm so glad you're alive.' My brother is awesome."

Beerman described the scene on the 53rd floor, where workers stopped to take count of colleagues before heading for the street far below. On the way down the stairs, those fleeing comforted each other and many used cell phones to call home. A woman who reached her husband passed the word: A plane had hit the building.

"We saw firefighters coming up the stairwell," Beerman said. "We felt kind of reassured."

Many firefighters would not make it out. Mayor Rudolph Giuliani was with a group of firefighters 10 minutes before they died, he said. "They were working very hard and they were working at what they loved to do."

Bill Hemm of Fayetteville, Ark., who was in New York for training at an investment firm at the World Trade Center, said he owes his life to police SWAT team members who prevented evacuees from going into areas of falling debris.

"Suffering breeds character, and character breeds faith, and in the end faith will prevail. This suffering has allowed, in the darkest hour, the light to shine most clearly." — Jesse Jackson

Bystanders cheer in support of rescue workers changing shifts near ground zero in New York.

"I know they died," he told *The Baxter Bulletin* of Mountain Home, Ark. "They had to have if they were still evacuating people. That's so sad. I guarantee they saved a bunch of lives."

Angelo Otchy sat on a curb near the Trade Center complex, head drooping after a long, long day. He'd arrived with other members of his New Jersey National Guard unit in the afternoon. In teams of two, they climbed up on the pile of rubble at One World Trade.

He and his partner dug and dug, using flashlights in the darkness, stopping only when ordered to withdraw, as Seven World Trade Center collapsed Tuesday night.

At the U.S. Capitol, dozens of House members gathered and heard Speaker Dennis Hastert, R-Ill., say, "We will stand as Americans together throughout this time."

The lawmakers then sang, "God Bless America."

"We will stand as Americans together throughout this time."

Doing God's Work

By AP Wire Service

He was known as Father Mike, the New York City Fire Department chaplain.

The Rev. Mychal Judge, 68, lived in the friary of the St. Francis of Assisi Church with his Franciscan brothers, across the street from Engine Co. One/Ladder Co. 24 in midtown Manhattan.

He used to sleep with a radio scanner in his room. Often, he ate in the firehouse. On Tuesday, Father Mike raced to the World Trade Center with the unit. The twin towers still were standing when he arrived.

He died when he paused to administer last rites to a firefighter mortally injured by a falling body from one of the 110-story towers.

"He took his hat off to pray, and something came down and hit him in the head," said retired Battalion Chief Bob McGrath.

On Thursday, firefighters and other mourners came to say goodbye to Father Mike, who was laid out in a coffin at the church wearing his brown monk's robe, his fire helmet by his side.

They remembered a favorite saying he'd use when firefighters asked his counsel:

"If you want to make God laugh," he would say, "tell him what you're doing tomorrow."

> *"I just think God wanted somebody to lead the guys to heaven."*
> —firefighter David Fullam on the loss of Father Mychal Judge

A tribute to Father Mike adorns the window of
Engine Co. One/Ladder Co. 24 in midtown Manhattan.

"America has suffered

a great loss, but what

has not been lost

is our spirit, our

resiliency as a society."

—Colin L. Powell

Americans Offer
Blood, Help, Prayers

By Russ Oates

NASHVILLE, Tenn. (AP)—Across the nation, Americans stood in line for hours to donate blood for terrorist attack victims, while doctors and rescue workers volunteered their help and many people offered prayers.

Reaction to the tragedies Tuesday ranged from shock and disbelief to anger, but there was a shared desire to lend assistance. Many literally rolled up their sleeves.

"I needed to do something, so that's why I'm here," said Steve Forslund, waiting to donate blood in Springfield, Mass.

At a mobile blood bank in Tampa, Fla., a line of more than 750 people snaked through a parking lot. In Denver the wait to give blood was six hours. In Phoenix, at least 400 people were turned away because there were too many for personnel to handle.

Roberta Toecker, who has been with the Red Cross in Nashville for 13 years, said she had never seen such a response in her city, even when a tornado struck in 1998. "This is just so shattering," she said.

Emergency personnel from coast to coast planned to join the relief effort, including 70 Phoenix firefighters and 65 members of a search-and-rescue team from the Seattle area.

The American Medical Association began compiling a list of doctors willing to volunteer. Some hospitals canceled elective surgeries to conserve medical supplies.

Shipments of blood from around the country were expected to begin arriving early Wednesday in New York, mostly by truck. A flight to transport blood from Denver early Wednesday received special clearance. Musicians and artists in the Phoenix area organized a benefit performance with proceeds going to victim relief. Actor Robin Williams was among hundreds giving blood in San Francisco.

Many churches held special services. More than 100 people gathered in Spokane's Riverfront Park for a noon prayer meeting that began with "Amazing Grace." Another 100 people showed up at a Seattle park to sing peace anthems. A noon Mass in Seattle attracted 1,200 worshippers, more than 10 times the norm.

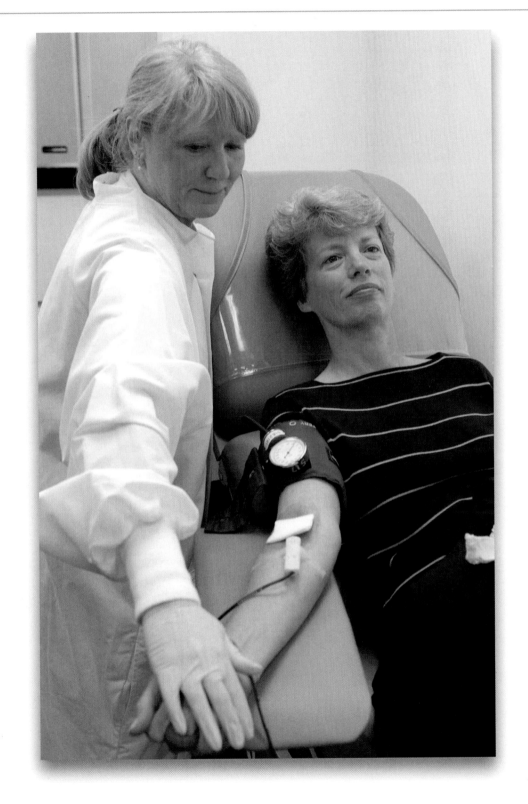

Ohio First Lady Hope Taft, right, gives blood in a bloodmobile outside the Ohio Statehouse Wednesday, Sept. 12, 2001.

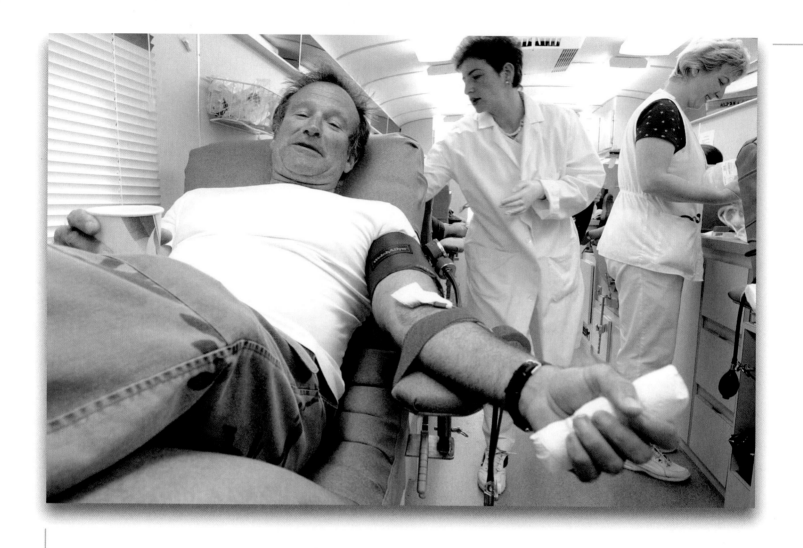

Gov. Rick Perry told University of Texas students at a candlelight vigil beneath the darkened university tower there was a great need for blood, plasma, clothes and money to help the thousands of victims. "It's a time to show our colors, to show our strengths, to show what holds us together as a nation," Perry said.

Hours earlier in downtown Dallas, hundreds of people lined up at Reunion Arena to donate blood. The scene was repeated in other Texas cities. "We have had hundreds of people come to our headquarters today," said Robin Davidson, public relations manager for Gulf Coast Regional Blood Center in Houston. "The wait is two and three hours long."

Those in the shadow of the World Trade Center disaster proved wrong the stereotypes about uncaring New Yorkers. Thousands lined up

"It's a time to show our colors, to show our strengths, to show what holds us together as a nation."

outside blood banks. People helped the elderly make their way out of buildings, and offered water to strangers with dust in their throats.

Ferry boats that carry commuters between Manhattan and New Jersey became rescue vessels for hundreds. After they crossed the Hudson River to Jersey City, volunteers greeted them with food and water. When a hotel near the ferry landing filled up, a luxury apartment complex across the street opened its doors, offering something to eat or a place to stay.

On the other side of the country, at Galloping Gerties restaurant near Fort Lewis, Wash., business was down and faces were solemn as customers and waitresses watched developments on TV. Owner Rod Mason gave free coffee to all soldiers in uniform.

Here Comes
the Bride

By The Associated Press

NEW YORK (AP)—With all that's happened in New York in the last week, Diane Gorumba's family didn't expect Mayor Rudolph Giuliani to keep his promise to walk her down the aisle.

But Giuliani kept his word Sunday, escorting the beaming bride and relishing a chance to put aside the World Trade Center horror, if only for a while.

The 23-year-old bride had asked the mayor to give her away after her firefighter brother, Michael Gorumba, died last month while fighting a blaze. Her father and grandfather died a year ago.

"We will go on. This proves it right here. The mayor came here—he thought about us," the newlywed said as she got into a limousine with her husband, Michael Ferrito, a police officer.

Giuliani, who has been working around the clock since the twin towers collapsed, said the wedding meant a great deal to him.

"It felt wonderful to be part of this," the mayor said. "This is what life is all about. You have to go on and take advantage of the good things in life."

"This is what life is all about. You have to go on and take advantage of the good things in life."

Rescue Workers
Describe Efforts

By Alan Clendenning and Sara Kugler

NEW YORK (AP)—Every once in a while, in the middle of the night and in the middle of a desperate search for survivors, a firefighter would suddenly stop, sit down and weep.

"The tears would just stream," said Alan Manevitz, a volunteer at the site of the World Trade Center disaster. "One guy threw up. You'd bring them a glass of water and they'd get back up and go to work."

The crews are getting through the horrific task because they are "guided, consciously and unconsciously, by their training to help save a life," said Manevitz, a psychiatrist from New York. "Even though they're tired and sad and angry, they're determined and still going forward with things.

"We go to such extremes to save even one life," he added.

A windy rain added to the awful conditions Friday, but workers said they were still driven by the hope of finding someone alive.

Volunteer Fred Medins, 46, of Bridgeport, Conn., said that several times during the night, would-be rescuers thought they might have heard faint cries for help from within the slippery, smelly pile of rubble.

Shouts went out for quiet and all digging stopped. But not once was there another sound.

"We'd hope we'd hear something," said Medins, a construction worker, after a soaking 12-hour shift. "I was saying to myself, 'Give us some sound. Give us some sound.'"

James Symington, a Halifax, Nova Scotia, constable who was searching with Tracker, a German shepherd trained to find survivors, said he thinks there is one more person alive: "That's what keeps me and everyone else going."

Dennis Gino, 22, of Bricktown, N.J., was working as a medic, flushing eyes and treating blisters. He marveled at the physical and emotional stamina of the police officers and firefighters among the rescue workers.

"We'd hope we'd hear something. I was saying
to myself, 'Give us some sound. Give us some sound.'"

AMERICA'S HEROES

"They're tired but they don't want to sleep because they just want to go right back out there and find people," he said. "There's firefighters and police in there still and they need to find them.

"It's like, sleep, wake up, go back out there," he said. "It's beautiful. It's a family working together."

Philip Lowenstein, 39, a fire department paramedic from New York, said his colleagues know the chances of finding anyone alive are fading.

"None of us would stop trying no matter what," he said. "But the reality is a little stark."

Michael Trovoni, a real estate man from Scarsdale, said he had been digging through the rubble with his hands. He described the smell of the pile as "burning, acrid, rubbery, metally."

He said workers found photographs, handwritten papers and ordinary items from workers' desktops. "It's someone's personal life, someone's personal effects, who's probably—may or may not be with us," he said. "It gives you pause."

"None of us would stop trying no matter what. But the reality is a little stark."

Pentagon Heroes
Knew What to Do

By Ron Kampeas

ARLINGTON, Va. (AP)—They believed they were in the most secure building in the strongest country in the world. Then a hijacked plane smashed into the Pentagon, their fortress. Yet they knew just what to do.

Knocked onto his back, Army Lt. Col. Victor Correa picked himself up from the floor and helped dazed colleagues out of the room. He headed for a wall of smoke down a hall littered with ceiling tiles, illuminated only by distant flames.

His big, booming voice was a natural to lead people to safety.

"I was screaming, 'Listen to me. Listen to me. Follow my voice,'" Correa recalled. "Folks started coming out."

Correa peered into the smoke, a water-soaked T-shirt pressed to his face. No one had to tell him what to do. "All of us had a different function, and I knew what mine was," he said.

All across the Pentagon, years of military training and discipline kicked in.

After an unfounded warning that a second aircraft was on its way, Correa forced open fire doors that had slammed shut. He went back in and started shouting again.

His shouting drew Carl Mahnken back to consciousness. Mahnken, a civilian in the army public affairs office, got up from the rubble-strewn floor and followed the voices through the smoke. Outside, he saw medics assisting the wounded. He ran over to help.

"You knew what to do, you ripped pants open, you took shoes off, you learned to help people with their shock, to get the blood flowing," said Mahnken, an Army reservist trained in first aid.

It was not until hours later, in the evening, that a firefighter told Mahnken about the golf-ball-size bump protruding from his crown. That was when he remembered his computer terminal flying toward his head, hours earlier.

"He gave me an ice pack," he said. "I hadn't noticed."

Marine Major Dan Pantaleo salvages a Marine Corps flag
that he found on the fourth level of the damaged area of the Pentagon.

"Listen to me. Listen
to me. Follow my voice."

Army Sgt. Maj. Tony Rose heard cries for help from behind a mountain of debris inside one room and set up a tunnel-digging team, working on rotation. One particularly hefty Navy Seal propped up the sagging ceiling.

"I forget his name," Rose said. "We just called him 'Big John.'"

They had helped seven people out through the impromptu tunnel when a wall buckled. They got out before it collapsed.

There was a call for volunteers in another area.

"There were some walking wounded, but everyone who could turned back," Rose said. "We had no maps, no flashlights, just wet T-shirts."

Some refused even to talk about themselves, insisting on recounting the heroism they witnessed.

Lt. Col. Sean Kelly singled out Army colleague Capt. Darrell Oliver. After Kelly and Oliver lifted a desk off a secretary, Oliver hoisted her onto his back and carried her out. Then he returned for a hearing impaired janitor who was sobbing in fear.

"He calmed him down, he carried him out over the partitions, over the furniture," Kelly said.

Kelly also noted National Guard Lt. Col. Larry Dudney, hacking from smoke inhalation as he lifted furniture off of his colleagues.

Each man said military training was key to the disciplined response—although each hastened to note that the civilians were also cool and resourceful.

"The thing with the military," Kelly said, "is that you ask for one volunteer, you get 50—you're trained for crisis."

Rose marveled as he recalled shouting orders at generals among the volunteers. "I sort of became the old sergeant major out there," he said. "People, regardless of rank, fell in and did what was needed."

Constantly on the rescuers' minds is the thought about what was left undone: 188 people believed dead from the plane and the Defense Department headquarters.

"I knew I had to leave when (the smoke) got worse. I think I did the right thing," Correa said.

"There are questions I'll have to live with for the rest of my life."

Some answers have already come: "I've been approached by several folks who said, 'That was the voice I heard.'"

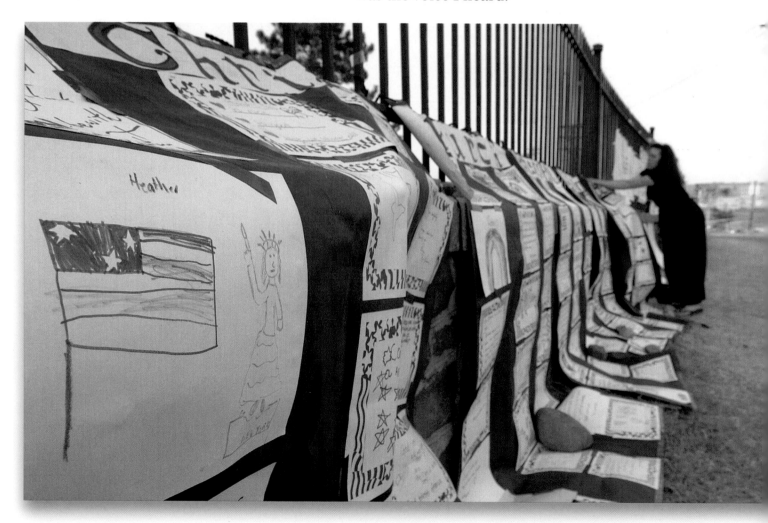

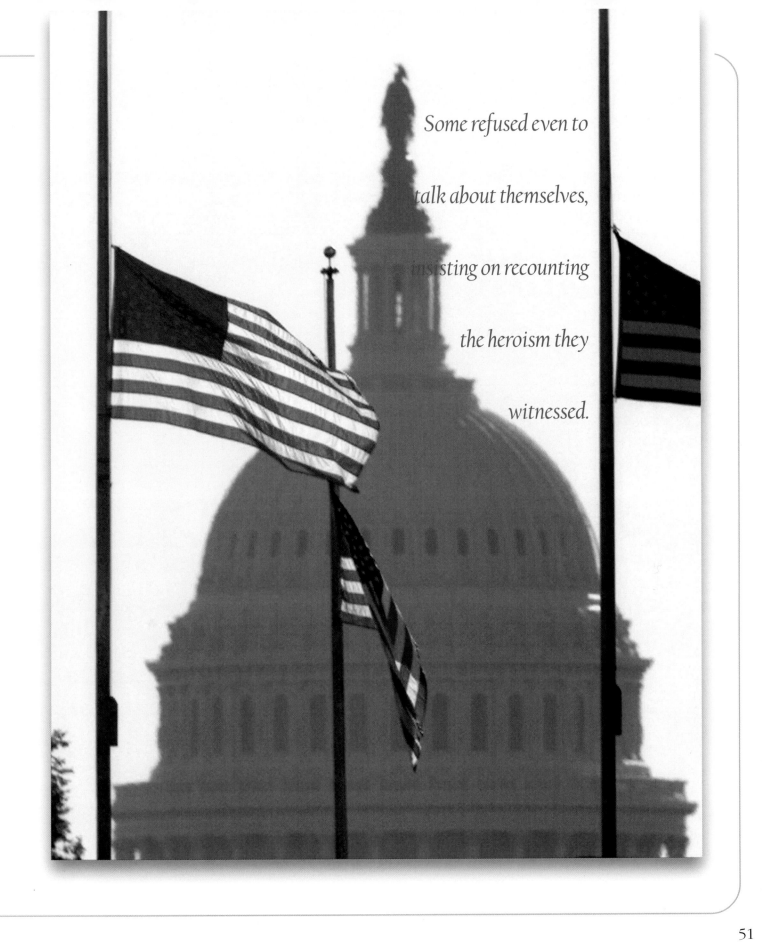

Some refused even to talk about themselves, insisting on recounting the heroism they witnessed.

"*We were shown tragedy ... and we were shown so many heroes.*"

—Monsignor Sal Criscuolo, District of Columbia police chaplain

Americans Open Wallets, Hearts

By Helen O'Neill

NEW YORK (AP)—She was wearing a mask and clutching her asthma inhaler. Her eyes, wide with fright, were caked with ash. Still, Collette Smith wouldn't have been anywhere else but digging through the rubble of the World Trade Center, volunteering her time and skills for the city she loves.

"It was like a mission," said the 32-year-old computer worker from the borough of Queens. It was just something I had to do."

All over the country, people felt the same. From the white-coated nurse wiping ash off an exhausted firefighter, to donors waiting hours to give blood, to corporations signing multimillion-dollar checks, America opened its wallets and hearts in an unprecedented outpouring of giving this week.

In business, in trades, in the arts, in schools, people have felt compelled to donate to relief efforts in New York and Washington. Contributions are so overwhelming and continue to come in so fast, that relief agencies can't begin to calculate them.

"We've all lost people, we've all lost something," said Richard Weiss of the Laborers International Union, which bused hundreds of hard-hatted volunteers to the site. The union, which represents 16,000 workers in New York City, also donated boxes of respirators, masks and work gear.

"We didn't do it as union members," Weiss said. "We did it because we are New Yorkers and human beings and because we just wanted to help."

In New Orleans, a TV station's on-the-street fund drive for victims of the attacks picked up $300,000 in cash in less than 24 hours—and the money was still pouring in. Children came with coin-filled piggy banks, and more than $1,000 was sent from the Guste public housing development, one of the city's poorest neighborhoods.

"People needed to do something," said WDSU-TV news director Margaret Cordes. "We can't just sit around and let terrorists take over our country."

"We can't be there on the front lines,
but like everyone else we wanted to help."

Hundreds of workers lined up outside the Jacob Javits Center in New York City to volunteer their services for the rescue effort.

In similar spirit, The Lilly Endowment in Indianapolis, the nation's second-largest foundation, pledged $30 million, the largest sum the endowment has ever donated to a relief effort. "We can't be there on the front lines, but like everyone else we wanted to help," said Gretchen Wolfram, spokesman for the foundation.

Other pledges from large corporations poured in: $10 million from General Electric Co., $10 million from Microsoft, $10 million from DaimlerChrysler, $5 million from Amerada Hess Corp., $3 million from Hewlett-Packard Co., $2 million from Wal-Mart Stores Inc. and $1 million from MGM Mirage Inc., the largest hotel-casino owner in Las Vegas.

Many of the announcements were accompanied by statements of appreciation for the bravery and courage of rescue workers in New York.

"The scope of the response has been unbelievable," said Dorothy Ridings, president of the Council on Foundations in Washington, D.C., which has been swamped with offers of help. "We've never seen a tragedy like this, and we've never seen donations like this."

Students at McKinley Thatcher elementary school in Denver wrote letters and drew pictures to send to New York students. One 8-year-old boy wrote, "I hope this picture makes you feel better. I will make a beautiful picture for you of the mountains so you can see what Denver's mountains look like."

In Chicago, people waited for hours to donate blood, bought sympathy cards for families of victims in New York and drove to the Empire State to volunteer their skills. "New York is kind of like a big brother to Chicago. Now the bigger, older brother got hurt and the little brother is helping out," said 26-year-old Eric Boyd as he waited in a two-hour line outside Chicago City Hall to give blood.

In Rochester, singer-songwriter Don McLean, who wrote the 1971 classic "American Pie," pledged $1 from each ticket sold to his show Saturday at the 2,900-seat Landmark Theater, while residents in nearby Canandaigua were arranging to send 500 home-baked apple pies to rescue teams. Pop diva Madonna resumed her regular tour schedule Thursday in Los Angeles, asking for a moment of silence for those killed and injured and pledging the proceeds from the show to help victims' families.

"It is absolutely astounding to me the overwhelming support all across the country of people wanting to do something," said Maj. Thomas Applin, the Salvation Army's emergency disaster coordinator for upstate New York.

"It is absolutely astounding to me the overwhelming support all across the country of people wanting to do something."

In Lake Forest, Ill., Abbott Laboratories, the second-largest U.S. supplier of hospital products, sent a convoy of supply trucks to New York and Washington-area hospitals. The company also arranged to send blood donations from Illinois in refrigerated trucks.

There were convoys rolling in from other parts, too.

The Kellogg Co. donated five truckloads of products. The Campbell Soup Co. sent caseloads of its V8 Splash drink. Ford Motor Co. and General Motors Corp. sent fleets of trucks, vans and sport utility vehicles to the disaster site.

And in northeast Kansas, the Prairie Band Potawatomi Nation donated $100,000 to the Red Cross relief effort with an oversized cardboard check that read: "Terrorist attack against the U.S."

"This is more than a donation of time or effort," said Walter Schaub, a volunteer firefighter from New Jersey, who drove from Columbus, Ohio, after his plane was stranded there. Slumped on the sidewalk, sweat and exhaustion pouring from his face after a day in the rubble, he gratefully accepted a bottle of water donated from a local deli.

"This is part of a brotherhood."

"This is more than a
donation of time or effort."

Terrorist Hunter's Final Mission

By AP Wire Service

John P. O'Neill was a hard-nosed, intrepid former FBI investigator who hunted terrorists around the world.

The 50-year-old O'Neill supervised the onsite investigations of the terrorist bombing of the USS Cole in Yemen last year and the deadly attacks on the U.S. embassies in Kenya and Tanzania in 1998.

O'Neill's Palm Pilot was filled with contacts he had accumulated in an FBI career that spanned three decades—beginning within days of his high school graduation.

He had a mind that could absorb a wealth of material very quickly. He was tireless—18-hour days were the norm—and dogged. Scotland Yard counterintelligence chief Alan Frye once said: "I wouldn't want to be the terrorist he was hunting. I've seen him move heaven and earth."

The dapper, 6-foot-2 O'Neill had retired only two weeks ago from his job as head of the FBI's national security division in New York to become director of security for the World Trade Center.

On Tuesday, he was in his 34th-floor office when the first of two hijacked planes hit the building. He phoned a son and a friend to reassure them he was fine.

He called FBI headquarters before re-entering one of the towers to help others. He was apparently inside when the buildings collapsed.

He has not been heard from since.

"*I wouldn't want to be the terrorist he was hunting. I've seen him move heaven and earth.*"

Americans
Raise Flags

By Pauline Arrillaga

Just Monday, town leaders in Amherst, Mass., voted to restrict how often and how long American flags could fly along downtown streets. In the words of the town manager, the displays seemed "a bit too much."

The next day, as the World Trade Center crumbled and the Pentagon burned, the banners were quickly hoisted once more on flagpoles lining two streets in the politically liberal town that is home to the University of Massachusetts. But now Old Glory flies at half-staff.

In the agonizing hours since terrorists stole thousands of lives and Americans' sense of security, one notion has been reinforced as never before: Americans have a deep-rooted, if sometimes dormant, sense of pride and patriotism.

Inquiries at military recruitment offices have swelled. Congressional members burst into "God Bless America" on the steps of the U.S. Capitol. E-mail writers declared Thursday "U.S. Color Day," a time for wearing red, white and blue.

And then there's Old Glory.

As the search and rescue effort continued amid the smoldering debris of the World Trade Center, workers said one symbol of survival helped them keep going: A flag had been planted in the rubble, "just to let them know that America's not dead," said firefighter Ronald Coyne.

Peter Buhrman's flag-making company in St. Louis, Mo., might get orders for 150,000 to 200,000 American flags on a busy day before a patriotic holiday. On Wednesday, he had nearly 2 million requests. By noon Thursday, another 750,000 poured in. "These are people basically saying I will take as many flags as you can send to me, and I don't care what size," Buhrman said.

In North Dakota, three flags are raised outside the home of retired policeman Craig Sjoberg. Peggy Ross, a sales clerk in an Albany, N.Y., jewelry store, put them inside the windows of her shop. In Bountiful, Utah, Boy Scouts helped hang them outside of homes.

And on the roof of the Pentagon, a huge banner of red, white and blue was draped

"We've seen the worst of what humanity can do, but now we're seeing the best."

Wednesday near the wall demolished by a hijacked plane in one of the terrorist attacks. The banner was hung for President Bush's visit.

Some, like Nevada real estate agent Virgil Ballard, gave them away. One by one, cars pulled up to the curb near Ballard's Reno realty office to grab one of 1,500 flags he had left over from a fund-raiser.

At the Colonial Flag and Specialty store in Sandy, Utah, customers clutching flags by the handful waited to pay for their purchases. Truck driver Bobby Whiteman planned to drape two flags from his rig's side mirrors. Don Rosenkrantz, a fire battalion chief, bought flags to hang on his fire truck. Even Martin Christensen, who has a flag flying outside his home, was in line. He wanted a bigger one.

"America needs, perhaps more than ever before, to unite in spirit—that will give us the strength to see us through this catastrophe," one e-mail note read.

In Grants Pass, Ore., the Caveman Kiwanis Club braved an early morning chill Wednesday to festoon lightposts with flags. Normally set out only on patriotic holidays, the flags were hung at the behest of bookstore owner Ruth McGregor.

McGregor got the idea after recalling her mother's response to Pearl Harbor: She immediately hoisted Old Glory on the front porch of their house.

"Most of the comments I've been getting are, 'God bless you, and God bless America.' Just over and over," she said.

"America needs, perhaps more than ever before, to unite in spirit—that will give us the strength to see us through this catastrophe."

Nurse Brings
Hope to Tragedy

By Larry Neumeister

NEW YORK (AP)—Nurse Donna Pritchard, knowing seconds save lives, stepped on the gas pedal when the first World Trade Center tower tumbled and shook the road beneath her car.

Fighting tears, Pritchard rushed from the borough of Brooklyn toward her job as the head of the surgery team of nurses at a Manhattan hospital.

More than 300 patients would pass through NYU Downtown Hospital that Tuesday, aided by people working a job that has lost its glamour with the young, creating a shortage of nurses nationwide.

The Brooklyn Bridge already closed, Pritchard raced to the nearby Manhattan Bridge, listening to the early radio reports and watching the other tower burn.

Streams of paper and dust from the collapse of the first tower fell across her car. She maneuvered downtown past limping survivors in the streets, some helped along by others.

As she rounded City Hall Park, the second tower crumbled. A mushroom cloud of gray debris chased her the last few hundred feet to the hospital.

"I couldn't see. I was covered in soot," she said. "My eyes were burning. As soon as I came in, they handed me water and a mask."

Her first patient was a man with a broken shoulder and cuts. The second was a woman struck by the landing gear of one of the planes that hit the towers. After multiple surgeries, the woman lived.

"When you see the patients, their wounds, you feel so much compassion for the people," said Pritchard, who has worked at the hospital for 20 years.

One man, Pritchard said, made it alive through a complex surgery only to die later. There was no time for grief.

"We did our best," she said.

"When you see the patients, their wounds,
you feel so much compassion for the people."

Another patient needed a pacemaker. With no telephones working to order the device, she ran onto the street and borrowed a cell phone from a passer-by. She got the pacemaker in time.

By Friday, she was feeling hopeful. She hopes the surge of enthusiasm to help others creates new interest in nursing, bringing a "positive outcome to a horrendous situation."

A nurse updates the family of a victim of the attacks on the World Trade Center. They were waiting in a staging area near ground zero.

"*We did our best.*"

"America is successful because of the hard work and creativity and enterprise of our people. These were the true strengths of our economy before September 11, and they are our strengths today."

—George W. Bush

Bush, Graham
Lead Prayer Service

By Sandra Sobieraj

WASHINGTON (AP)—President Bush and the Rev. Billy Graham led four former presidents and the nation in prayer Friday, declaring America united by a "kinship of grief and a steadfast resolve" to defeat terrorism.

Former presidents Gerald Ford, Jimmy Carter, George H.W. Bush and Bill Clinton surrounded their successor in the front pews. The president, arriving with first lady Laura Bush, appeared to fight tears as he greeted his father with a quick handshake.

"Our unity is a kinship of grief and a steadfast resolve to prevail against our enemies," Bush said. "And this unity against terror is now extended across the world."

The Rev. Billy Graham, a longtime counselor to American presidents, prayed that the country would "feel the loving arms of God wrapped around us" but told Americans it was all right to be angry. "You may even be angry with God. I want to assure you that God understands these feelings that you have," said Graham, 82.

"Yes, our nation has been attacked. . . . But now we have a choice whether to implode and disintegrate emotionally and spiritually as a people and a nation, or whether we choose to become stronger through all of the struggle to rebuild on a solid foundation."

Bush, too, spoke in healing tones, praising rescue workers and people who sacrificed their lives to save others in the attacks on the World Trade Center and the Pentagon. "This nation is peaceful but fierce when stirred to anger," Bush said.

With all of the Cabinet secretaries, Supreme Court justices, congressional leadership and former presidents assembled under one roof, Vice President Cheney did not appear. The Secret Service had spirited the vice president, first in line to succeed Bush in the event of catastrophe, to the secluded safety of Camp David on Thursday afternoon.

Flight 93 Heroes
Heard Before Crash

By Joann Loviglio

PHILADELPHIA (AP)—"Are you guys ready? Let's roll!" is an expression Todd Beamer used whenever his wife and two young sons were leaving their home for a family outing.

The 32-year-old businessman and Sunday school teacher said the same thing before he and other passengers apparently took action against hijackers aboard United Airlines Flight 93, shortly before the plane crashed in a western Pennsylvania field.

Todd Beamer placed a call on one of the Boeing 757's on-board telephones and spoke for 13 minutes with GTE operator Lisa D. Jefferson, Beamer's wife, Lisa, said. He provided detailed information about the hijacking and said he and others on the plane were planning to act against the terrorists aboard.

Then he asked Jefferson to promise she would call his wife of seven years—who is expecting a third child—and their two sons, ages 1 and 3. After receiving clearance from investigators, Beamer said Jefferson kept her promise.

Todd Beamer dropped the phone after talking to Jefferson, leaving the line open. It was then that the operator heard Beamer's words: "Let's roll."

Then silence.

Several other passengers made phone calls from the jet before it crashed southeast of Pittsburgh: Thomas Burnett Jr., 38; Mark Bingham, 31; and Jeremy Glick, 31. Glick and Burnett said they were going to do something.

"He wanted me to recite the Lord's Prayer with him. He recited the Lord's Prayer from start to finish."

— Lisa Jefferson, GTE operator

David, Andrew and Lisa Beamer sit near a photo of their father and husband, Todd Beamer.

"He was the best father I could ever imagine for my boys. When he opened the door at night it was like a rampage to see who could get to the door first."

—Lisa Beamer

Thomas Burnett, Jr.

> *"I'll tell my children the kind of life he led with honor and dignity and integrity and how he believed that being a good citizen was the most important thing any of us could become."*
>
> —Deena Burnett

Burnett and his wife, Deena, had three conversations over his cell phone before the plane crashed. Deena said that Tom asked a lot of questions about the attacks on the World Trade Center, then she heard him and other passengers formulate a plan to thwart the hijackers.

Deena and Tom exchanged "I love you's," but no "good-bye's." Deena believes that Tom thought he was coming home.

Whether it was racing across traffic to save a wayward child, running with the bulls in Pamplona, or helping a neighbor fix her telephone, Mark Bingham was ready.

The enthusiasm and strength of the brawny, 6-foot-4 rugby player leave no doubt in the minds of family and friends that, if Bingham was able, he was likely among those who tried to thwart hijackers from aiming Flight 93 at a heavily populated area.

"He was this physically imposing, but incredibly compassionate and intelligent man, who would not have stood by and let terrorists kill thousands more people," said Bryce Eberhart, a teammate on Bingham's rugby team.

"Mark," said friend Brian Johnson, "was a hero in everyday life."

Lisa Jefferson, the 911 operator who spoke with Todd Beamer on Flight 93:

"He said, in case I don't make it through this, would you please do me a favor and call my wife and my family and let them know how much I love them. He told me he has two boys, David and Andrew. Then he said his wife is also expecting. So we talked.

"When the plane was flying erratic he thought he had lost conversation with me. And he was hollering in the phone, 'Lisa, Lisa.' And I said, 'I'm still here Todd. I'm still here. I'm not going anywhere, I'll be here as long as you will.'

"After that he had a sigh in his voice, he took a deep breath. He was still holding the phone but he was not talking to me, he was talking to someone else. And I can tell that he had turned away from the phone to talk to someone else. And he said, 'You ready? OK. Let's roll.'"

Moments later, screams, commotion.

"Then it went silent. I didn't hear anything else from him. I kept the phone line open for about 15 minutes, hoping he would come back to the phone. I was calling his name. He never came back to the phone. About 10 minutes later, we had heard that the plane had crashed in Pittsburgh and I knew that was his plane. It was United flight 93."

Deena Burnett: "The phone rang in on call waiting and it was Tom. I asked him immediately if he was OK and he said no. He said I'm on the airplane, United Flight 93 and it's been hijacked.

"He said, we can't wait for the authorities. And he was just pumping me for information. His adrenaline was flowing. And he was trying to sort it out. And I think he realized much sooner than I did that it was a suicide mission.

"And he said, 'OK, there's a group of us and we're going to do something.' I said, 'No.' And I said, 'Please sit down and be still, be quiet, don't draw attention to yourself.' And he said, no, he said, 'If they're going to drive this plane into the ground,' he said, 'We've got to do something.'

"He was taking down information, he was planning what they were going to do. And he was not interested in reviewing his life, or whispering sweet nothings to the telephone, I assure you. He was problem solving and he was going to take care of it and come on home."

He never called back.

"I was still holding on to the telephone. I held on to the phone for three hours until the battery ran down."

Passenger Jeremy Glick, 31, telephoned his wife Liz, after terrorists took over, Glick's uncle Tom Crowley said. Liz conferenced the call to a 911 dispatcher, who told Glick about the New York attacks.

"Jeremy and the people around them found out about the flights into the World Trade Center and decided that if their fate was to die, they should fight," Crowley said. "At some point, Jeremy put the phone down and simply went and did what he could do."

California Senator Barbara Boxer presents an American flag to Mark Bingham's partner, Paul Holm.

"*Mark was a hero in everyday life.*"

Bingham's parents, Jerry and Karen Bingham, following a news conference.

Jeremy Glick and his daughter, Emerson.

"Call my wife and family and let them know how much I love them."

Lisa Beamer hugs a friend
after her husband's memorial service.

"Today is a day to renew our faith in America."

—Bob Taft, Ohio Governor

Support for
Pentagon Rescue Workers

By Jennifer Loven

WASHINGTON (AP)—A small city has sprung up at a Pentagon parking lot to offer hot food, clean clothes and comforting conversation to those enduring the grim task of combing the rubble on the other side of the crippled building.

"Some of them are having some real problems," said Ronald Hester of Ashboro, N.C., one of 37 Baptists from North Carolina who are handling most of the cooking and feeding chores. "Our people will just sit down and talk with them, and then they go back to work."

At the compound are trucks full of underwear and shirts for the search and rescue workers. Under a Red Cross tent they can get treatment for minor injuries. Nearby is a McDonald's truck in the shape of a hamburger bun.

Peter DePuy and Rudy Eversburg were part of the first teams to respond Tuesday when a hijacked airliner slammed into the Defense Department headquarters. It was pandemonium then, almost workmanlike numbing, the Arlington, Va., firefighters said.

"Every time when you have a chance to sit down and think about it some more, it really hits you," Eversburg said.

"If you're focused on your job and you're trying to do your job, it's kind of a salvation," he said. "No matter how horrific it may get, the thought of not going in and doing the job never enters your mind."

Members of a military mortuary unit, who retrieve remains spotted by recovery workers, said they could take satisfaction knowing they were bringing some closure to victims' families.

Artwork by students from Crossfield Elementary in
Oak Hill, Va. decorate Comfort City and show support for Pentagon rescuers.

Ship Offers Bed,
Shower for N.Y. Crew

By Michael Hill

ABOARD USNS COMFORT (AP)—The first thing Tom Chico did was take a shower. Then he finally got to sleep in a comfortable bed.

The Air National Guard sergeant is among hundreds of World Trade Center disaster workers who have unwound aboard this 894-foot U.S. Navy hospital ship docked off Manhattan.

The USNS Comfort offers what workers spending grueling hours around the destroyed buildings want: a hot meal, fresh clothes, a pillow.

On Monday, Chico and two fellow soldiers deployed from the Albany, N.Y., area for security details, picked up mouthwash, sweatshirts and shaving cream—small items that made a big difference to them.

"This is great," Chico said. "We have someplace to call home here."

Added Sgt. Michael Woodcock: "It's like the Hilton."

Not exactly.

The 44,648-ton Comfort is more like a tanker, which it was before it was turned into a floating hospital for the Navy. Outside, the ship's pure white paint job is interrupted only by giant red medical crosses. Inside, the accommodations are decidedly military.

The beds are bunks stacked three high. Hot dishes like chicken, rice and cauliflower are served from a steam table. A cornucopia of donated freebies for the workers—from shoes to peanuts to Bibles—are laid out on unused beds.

Spartan or not, it is appreciated by out-of-town soldiers, firefighters and police officers working around the clock amid the dust and rubble. Some of the guard members on board the Comfort on Monday had been sleeping in armories or tents. Others, like Air National Guard Sgt. Dean Trumbull, brought too few changes of clothes. He spent time Monday checking bins for the right size underwear.

"These guys that come on board, we recharge their batteries," Capt. Ed Nanartowich said. "And then they get back to doing the heroic work that they do."

The Comfort shipped out of Baltimore on Wednesday without the crew knowing whether

The USNS Comfort offers what workers spending grueling hours around the destroyed buildings want: a hot meal, fresh clothes, a pillow.

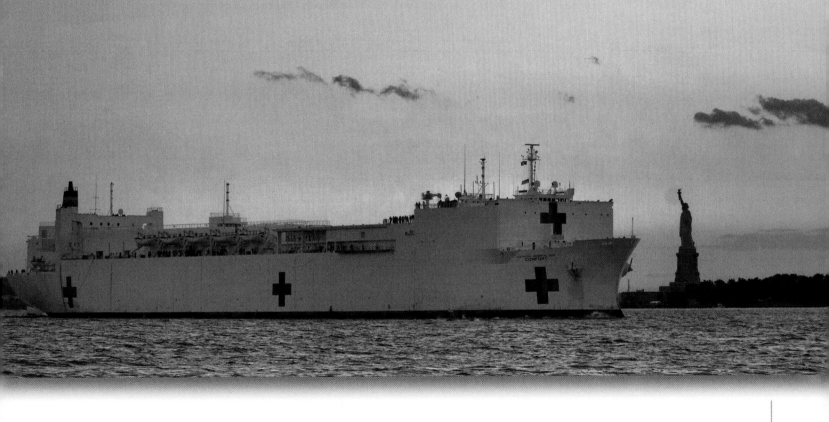

they would be staffing a hospital, transport ship or morgue. The order to become a floating respite center came on the way to New York.

Docked on the Hudson River several miles from the disaster site, more than a thousand military and civilian workers have checked in around the clock since Friday for a meal, a rest or other services such as laundry.

"We don't stop," said Melissa Zanvettor as she worked the food line. "It's 24 hours."

The Comfort has been deployed many times since being delivered to the Navy in 1987, notably during the Gulf War. It has 12 operating rooms and can receive 200 patients a day.

"These guys that come on board, we recharge their batteries. And then they get back to doing the heroic work that they do."

"We don't stop. It's 24 hours."

Firefighters Promoted
to Fill Gap

By Matt Crenson

NEW YORK (AP)—New York promoted 168 firefighters on Sunday, and no one laughed or beamed with pride. There was only heartache.

These were the replacements for a Fire Department command structure that was eviscerated in a few moments on Tuesday morning, when the World Trade Center toppled. Their promotions were a necessity, not a joy.

"No one really wants to be here. No one really wanted to be promoted," said Jerry Horton, who became a captain during the ceremony.

With nearly 300 firefighters lost beneath the jumbled remains of the twin towers, Mayor Rudolph Giuliani compared the promotions to battlefield commissions awarded during wartime.

"We are shaken, but we are not defeated," said Fire Commissioner Thomas Von Essen. "We stare adversity in the eye and we move on."

Von Essen delivered his remarks in a strong, unwavering voice, but his face twisted in pain the moment he finished. He collapsed into a chair on the stage and hung his head as Giuliani stepped to the podium.

Giuliani hailed the firefighters as heroes, then helped swear the promoted into their new positions.

Some of the men were not there. Some of them were still under the wreckage of the Trade Center, their promotions a gesture of faith that they and some of their brethren will survive.

The men awaited their honors in a plaza adjacent to the department's Brooklyn headquarters, sitting stoically under the same azure skies that delivered death to their colleagues five days ago.

The promotions reached all the way to the top. Chief of Operations Daniel A. Nigro was named Chief of Department, the highest uniformed position in the organization. He replaces Peter Ganci, the former department chief, who died in Tuesday's attacks and was buried Saturday.

After the ceremony the firefighters chatted quietly with their families. One man tousled his son's hair. Another lifted his daughter to his

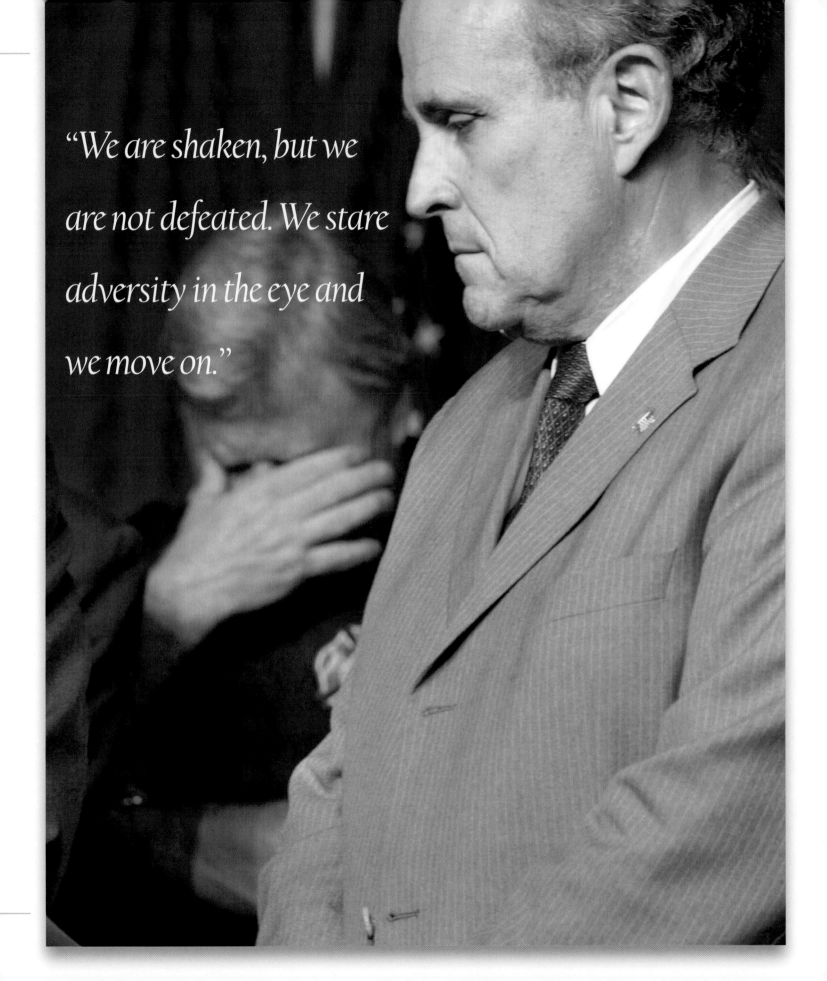

"We are shaken, but we are not defeated. We stare adversity in the eye and we move on."

New York City Batallion 39 Chief Bob Keys, left, shares a tearful hug with his brother,
Tim, who was promoted following the tragic loss of fire personnel during the collapse of the World Trade Center.

shoulders. A few posed for snapshots, their faces pale and their smiles thin-lipped.

This thought was never far from anyone's mind: Less than two miles away, hundreds of their comrades remained entombed beneath a mountain of twisted steel and crumbled concrete.

So far only 18 of the 300 fire department personnel thought to have been lost in the disaster are confirmed dead.

"I need you all to go out there and to help us do the very best we can to get our guys," Von Essen said.

The New York Fire Department is accustomed to burying its own. A memorial at its Brooklyn headquarters names more than 750 firefighters who have fallen in the line of duty since the department was formed in 1865.

Never have so many been lost at one time. With 11,400 firefighters on the force, one out of every 38 is either dead or missing. Almost every station house has been touched by the tragedy.

Yet even after suffering such heavy casualties, both department officials and the rank-and-file said they are confident they can keep doing their jobs. Under normal conditions, most of those elevated Sunday would have been promoted in the next six to eight months anyway.

"We're always ready," said Anthony Rocco, who was promoted to lieutenant.

"We're always ready."

"*Now, we know what's really important are the people we love, and our country.*"

—Laura Bush,
First Lady

America Mourns
With Flags, Candles

By Rachel Zoll

A country in mourning poured its grief into prayer and defiant chants, showing unity in the flicker of thousands of candles at vigils across America.

As dusk fell on a day of remembrance, strangers congregated a few miles from the devastation in New York and they gathered as far away as Alaska to show solidarity. On the Las Vegas Strip, the lights went down.

About 500 people joined together Friday night at Denver's Washington Park, holding candles and softly singing "Amazing Grace" and "America the Beautiful."

"I brought my 6-year-old here tonight because it's important that she knows there are more good people in the world than bad," said Terra Avila, 29, of Denver.

About 75 people lighted candles in a park on Seattle's Queen Anne Hill as the sun set behind the Olympic Mountains. The crowd had a clear view of the Space Needle, topped by an American flag at half-staff.

Anne Gauthier, 28, an executive assistant at Microsoft Corp., said she came out "to say yes, you have hurt us more deeply than you ever did before, but you're not going to break us."

About 2,500 candles lined a marble balcony and the steps of the Rhode Island Statehouse, illuminating the lawn of the historic building where thousands gathered for a nighttime service.

Ed and Tracy Berry and their two young children lighted five candles on their quiet street in north Dallas, responding to e-mails sent by their church and a friend.

"We told our 5-year-old that a terrible accident had happened and lots of people are hurt," Ed Berry said.

On Manhattan's Upper West Side, hundreds met at a Mexican restaurant that handed out candles and flags. People cheered and sang "God Bless America" as military jets flew overhead.

"I brought my 6-year-old here tonight because it's important that she knows there are more good people in the world than bad."

"I've been in the house for the last three days in shock. This is my first day out," said Millie Cintron, a Wall Street worker who saw the Trade Center towers collapse.

A widespread Internet message had urged people to light candles Friday to "show the world that Americans are strong and united together against terrorism."

President Bush had called for the day of remembrance to memorialize the victims of Tuesday's terrorist attacks at the World Trade Center and Pentagon.

"You realize that being a Democrat, Republican, New Yorker or from Los Angeles doesn't matter. Today from this day on, everybody is just an American."

At the Oklahoma City National Memorial, the site of the 1995 bombing of the Alfred P. Murrah Federal Building, several hundred people sang under an American elm that survived that blast.

Outside Los Angeles' city hall, Arlene Mills, 40, and her husband wore red, white and blue bandanas and carried a sign that read "God Bless America. R.I.P. Victims of Terrorists."

Tears flowed from behind Mills' dark sunglasses.

"You realize that being a Democrat, Republican, New Yorker or from Los Angeles doesn't matter," she said. "Today from this day on, everybody is just an American."

"…show the world that Americans are strong and united …"

Man's Best Friend

Countless inspiring stories of human rescue and sacrifice continue to surface in the wake of the World Trade Center recovery effort.

Dedicated experts from the rescue community, including structure specialists, heavy riggers who work with cranes, communications experts, building planning teams, medical rescue personnel and numerous volunteers, work up to 18 hours a day at ground zero in the hopes of saving even one more precious life.

Taking few breaks and resting on cots and in makeshift tents, these tireless workers have gotten no more than four to six hours of sleep at any given time and are suffering from physical and mental exhaustion.

Another team of dedicated and exhausted searchers is the rescue dogs employed to comb through the mountains of debris to determine if any life is present.

"The firemen find a hole for us that there could be a possible survivor, and then the dog goes down into the hole," said Joe Palfrey, a police officer from Lebanon, Ill., who arrived in New York on Wednesday after driving straight through to volunteer his services.

These dedicated dogs are also working up to 18 hours a day. At the World Trade Center scene, 200 of them have needed veterinary treatment since the attack, mostly for heat and exhaustion. The trained MASH unit on the scene has never experienced this kind of volume before.

"It's unbelievable," said Chief Roy Gross with the Suffolk County SPCA. "Sometimes they come in 15 at a time."

The dogs and the handlers are partners. Chief Gross has witnessed unparalleled determination from them every day, even when the dogs are sick and tired.

"I had one handler in here the other day," he said. "The dog was pulling him back to the pile. The dog had that scent on him. He knew there was something there."

Like many handlers, Erick Robertson of Oakhurst, Cal., brought his one-year-old search and rescue dog, Porkchop, to the SPCA mobile clinic for a dehydration intravenous treatment.

Erick Robertson with his rescue dog, Porkchop.

"These dogs put their lives on the line for the people they're trying to rescue."

They had been working together for days at the recovery scene.

Nearby, volunteers petted a Belgian shepherd named Tochka, which was so depleted after a day and a half of searching for survivors, she just laid down among the wreckage.

While these remarkable rescue dogs are trained for these types of missions, they are still vulnerable to injuries, especially from glass and debris, which is rough on their paws. Humans are able to pay attention to what they are stepping on and look for sharp objects that might cause injury. The dogs, because they are so involved in their work, are more likely to sustain injuries in hazardous areas.

Several companies have responded to the need to protect the K-9 units' paws from splintered glass and debris while they continue their search. A Canadian company, Muttlucks, Inc., supplies boots for dogs working in many disaster situations, and sent hundreds of pairs to the New York City Police Department. The boots resemble socks but have padded soles to protect the paws and Velcro straps that fit around the ankles.

"These dogs will work until they drop."

"Those dogs put their lives on the line for the people they're trying to rescue. They're no different from police and firemen. They need protective gear too," said Marianne Bertrand, the firm's owner. "The dogs will work until they drop. We're elated to be able to do something."

Husky Express in Cora, Wyo., a company that makes dog-sledding supplies, also provided the heavy-duty boots for the dogs searching the rubble. "We sent every bootie we had. Finished booties, booties we had for our personal use, everything," said Kathie Jacobson, co-owner of the company.

Dog Leads
Blind Man to Safety

WESTFIELD, N.J. (AP)—Mike Hingson, who is blind, made his way to safety from the 78th floor of the World Trade Center during the terrorist attacks, thanks to Roselle, his 3 1/2-year-old yellow Labrador guide dog.

"Roselle did a good job," said Hingson, 51. "She stayed focused. We stayed to the side. We smelled a lot of jet fuel on the way down. . . . Some people had a lot of problems breathing."

The first airliner in the attacks struck the north tower where Hingson worked as a sales manager at Quantum ATL, a network data-storage company.

He and colleague Dave Frank rounded up six employees of another company who were there for a meeting, and pointed them toward the stairs. Then Hingson grabbed his briefcase, and he, Frank and Roselle headed down.

It took a half hour to walk down to the ground floor. Once outside, Frank told Hingson both towers were on fire. They ran as the south tower came down in a huge cloud, and they soon heard the north tower collapse.

They walked north for about 10 minutes, when Hingson called his wife, Karen, on his cell phone. He said simply, "It's me."

By 7 p.m., Hingson and Roselle had taken a train back home to New Jersey. "She never hesitated," Hingson said as the dog lay by his feet. "She never panicked."

There are bursts of adrenaline when the dogs from the K-9 search units pick up a scent, known as "making a hit." K-9 unit officer Robert Schnelle, working with his dog, Atlas, noted that even though no survivors had been found for quite a while, the teams were still in search-and-rescue mode.

The animals become discouraged if they go for long periods of time without finding any survivors. To combat this, the dogs' handlers take turns hiding for each others' dogs so they can experience some success.

"Doing a live find," says handler Deresa Teller, "helps build a dog's confidence."

Schnelle said that Atlas seemed affected by his failure to find survivors but that his presence helped hearten rescuers. "Atlas is a little diversion. They like to pet the dog. It gives them a smile," he said.

Another team of dedicated and exhausted searchers is the rescue dogs.

Rescue Teams
Relieved at Pentagon

By David Pace

WASHINGTON (AP)—Ian decorated his note with a heart and an American flag.

"Somewhere in America, a little boy or girl is counting on you to rescue their parents, and I know you will," he wrote to Pentagon rescue workers.

The letter was among the hundreds that were sent by schoolchildren and now are in boxes inside a support area in the Pentagon's south parking lot. That's where workers take a break from the wreckage for some rest and food.

Teams from Fairfax County, Va., and Montgomery County, Md., first on the scene after the hijacked airliner crashed Sept. 11, were being replaced by a search and rescue unit from New Mexico. "Certainly it takes a toll on the men and workers in there," said Tom Carr, leader of the Montgomery County task force. "We have to admit that."

But Carr described the rotation of search crews as standard practice for a prolonged effort like this. He said the reduction in the number of crews at the Pentagon of four to three indicates that work to stabilize the damaged building is nearly complete.

In the support area for Pentagon rescue workers, circus-sized tents provide fast food and counselors for the weary.

Damon Maclin, 36, of Memphis, Tenn., said he's looking forward to his team being relieved later this week so he can return home and see his 7-year-old twin daughters.

"They'll get a big hug and a kiss—a long one," he said.

Maclin was in a group of about a half-dozen rescuers, their faces smudged with soot and dirt, sitting around a table eating lunch.

Asked if there were any special moments or images any of them will take back to Tennessee, Tony Redwine welled up with tears and said, "I don't want to talk about that."

Jerry Crawford, who heads the Tennessee search unit, said many of the crew members have asked to see clergy.

"Somewhere in America a little boy or girl is counting on you to rescue their parents, and I know you will."

"They've had a major lifetime experience that none of them will ever get out of their minds," he said.

What workers were eager to discuss, however, was the camaraderie the search teams, both here and in New York, have developed over the years training and working together at disaster sites like this.

Kenny Jackson said he knew at least one of the firefighters who died in New York and is looking forward to going up there to help in the effort.

"Not only to help them, but to be there with them," he said. "It's hard for us to even comprehend what they're going through up there."

In a part of the support area closer to the crash site sits a memorial the Defense Department set up for family members of Pentagon workers killed in the attack. The memorial is a four-by-eight-foot platform with a three-foot-high board on which family members have pinned photos of missing loved ones, notes and personal items.

Army Col. Richard Breen said nearly 500 family members have visited the memorial in the last two nights.

"It's been hard, but they're grateful for the opportunity," he said.

"They've had a major lifetime experience
that none of them will ever get out of their minds."

Members of the Fort Meyer Army Band perform for rescue workers in Comfort City at the Pentagon.

First Lady
Visits Injured

By Lawrence L. Knutson

WASHINGTON (AP)—First lady Laura Bush on Wednesday visited three hospitalized military personnel who leaped to safety immediately after a hijacked jetliner flew into the Pentagon.

Mrs. Bush also thanked White House employees who lined up to donate blood under the ornate ceilings of the Executive Office Building's Indian Treaty Room.

At Walter Reed Army Medical Center, Mrs. Bush visited the three injured service members, then thanked members of the hospital's emergency response team who rushed to help after the jetliner exploded inside the Pentagon.

Speaking briefly to reporters, she offered sympathy to the victims of the terrorist attacks, both at the Pentagon and at the World Trade Center in New York.

"All of us now in America have a chance to show our resilience and our courage," Mrs. Bush said, standing at the hospital's emergency entrance.

An opportunity has opened, she said, "to do what we can for our fellow Americans, to think how we can help each other and to reassure our young children . . . .

"Let them know they are safe and are loved," the first lady said.

"All of us now in America have a chance to show our resilience and our courage."

"People are looking for heroes and finding them in firefighters."

—Jill Stein, sociologist

Internet Helps
Propel Donations

By Anick Jesdanun

NEW YORK (AP)—Charities have already collected more than $200 million for victims of the terrorist attacks, much of it spurred by the ease of donating over the Internet.

Many charity officials believe that the amount raised for victims of the Sept. 11 catastrophe will eclipse the total collected after other major disasters, including the 1995 Oklahoma City bombing.

America Online has been greeting its subscribers with a special window outlining ways to donate. EBay began a "$100 million in 100 days" campaign. Amazon.com and Yahoo are collecting money for major charities.

The International Association of Fire Fighters received several million dollars for families of the hundreds of firefighters believed killed. Spokesman George Burke credited the many Web sites that created links to the fund.

"We've all had that intention to do something, but the bucket wasn't there or the checkbook was in the next room," said Dorothy Ridings, president of the Council on Foundations, which formed The September 11th Fund with United Way and the New York Community Trust. In Washington, President Bush asked Americans to be generous.

"There are challenges that remain for those who suffer today," Bush said. "We've got a lot of work to do as a nation, and these good efforts, these good charitable compassionate efforts, need the full support of Americans everywhere."

Dozens of charitable efforts have blossomed to cope with last week's attacks in New York and Washington. To ease bureaucratic tangles, the Internal Revenue Service announced it would speed up approval of new requests for tax-exempt status.

At the American Red Cross, spokeswoman Devorah Goldburg called giving levels unprecedented. Nearly 40 percent of the $118 million it received or had pledged came over the Internet.

"These good charitable compassionate
    efforts need the full support of Americans everywhere."

Tyson Corporation employees roast hundreds of pounds of donated chicken in the 5-acre "Comfort City" to feed rescue workers at the Pentagon.

The September 11th Fund also collected more than $100 million in cash and pledges. The amount includes several large grants, including $10 million each from the Lilly Endowment and Microsoft.

Maj. Gary Miller of the Salvation Army estimates that $2 million of the $4 million it raised came over the Internet.

"*Life presents as many opportunities for happiness as it does for tragedy.*"

—Rudolph Giuliani

New York's Mayor
Shines in Adversity

By Beth Harpaz

NEW YORK (AP)—Mayor Rudolph Giuliani has been quoting Winston Churchill to help New York get through its darkest hour.

Now, even the mayor's usual critics say his steady leadership since the terrorist attack on the World Trade Center has been Giuliani's finest hour.

After barely escaping with his own life from a building adjacent to the twin towers, he gently, calmly informed his fellow New Yorkers that the death toll would be "more than any of us could bear." He lost personal friends and officiated at funerals; he has worked around the clock, holding news conferences in between visits to the disaster site and meetings to coordinate the response; he has pledged to rebuild and prosper; and he even found time to officiate at a wedding, saying, "This is what life is all about."

Many New Yorkers are now wishing they could undo a term-limits law that prevents the lame-duck mayor—who has just three months left in office—from running for office again. "Ten more years!" shouted a rescue worker Monday as Giuliani toured the site of the World Trade Center disaster.

Giuliani's new admirers include diehard Democrats who never voted for him, activists who have long lambasted, and people in other countries who may not have known his name a week ago. Political consultants say Giuliani could run for anything now and win.

Giuliani deflected the acclaim. "What I should do is do the job until Dec. 31, and prepare someone else as the next mayor," he said.

"I wish he could stay on and that we didn't have term limits," said Linda Yarwood, a Manhattan paralegal. "I would vote for him again. He is a pillar of strength for our community and our nation."

Nelson Warfield, a Republican political consultant and former press secretary to Bob Dole, predicted that "whoever becomes mayor will beg him to stay on in some role to oversee the rebuilding of the city. But I think Rudy Giuliani

"*Giuliani could run for anything now and win.*"

goes wherever he wants from here. If he chooses to seek political office, I can't imagine anybody stopping him."

Four Democrats and two Republicans are running for mayor. The primary was supposed to have taken place Sept. 11, the day two hijacked jets crashed into the Trade Center. The primary was rescheduled for Sept. 25.

In an interview with Barbara Walters to air Monday night on ABC, Giuliani recommended that people read "about the Battle of Britain and how the people of London lived through the constant daily bombardment by the Nazis. . . . They never gave up their spirit, and they figured out how to go about their lives."

Randy Mastro, who heads a commission on the City Charter, which bars officials from serving more than two terms, said he has received hundreds of calls and e-mails "asking if there's anything that can be done to see to it that Rudy continues as mayor." But Mastro said that even as a write-in candidate, Giuliani could not legally serve unless the City Council or the state Legislature changed the term limits law.

New York Mayor Rudolph Giuliani, President Bush and New York Governor George Pataki inspect ground zero.

Yankees Moved
by Visit to Families

By Josh Dubow

NEW YORK (AP)—Bernie Williams and his New York Yankees teammates walked anxiously into the armory where people gathered for news of their loved ones missing after last week's terrorist attacks at the World Trade Center.

Unsure what to say to the grieving people, Williams was brought to one woman searching for a missing family member and said the only thing he could: "It looks like you need a hug."

The two embraced and the woman started crying.

"It was a very tough situation," Williams recalled Sunday. "It was one of those things I'll never forget."

Many of the Yankees took a tour of the city Saturday night, visiting the armory, a staging area for weary rescue workers, and a hospital where doctors were waiting to treat injured survivors who never came. It was the first time many of them had made it anywhere close to the scene of Tuesday's attacks.

"I sort of feel a little more useful now," manager Joe Torre said. "That is the only way to describe it.

"We went there not knowing how we would be received. We left there knowing it was a very important stop for us."

All of the Yankees who made the trip downtown Saturday were indelibly moved by the sights and people they saw.

Most memorable was the wall of pictures of the missing people outside the armory—less than three miles north of where the twin towers once stood.

"It hits you square in the face," Scott Brosius said. "Every one of those people is in a place we hope we will never have to be."

The players sensed that their visit brought a rare smile to the families and rescue workers who have had little to be happy about since Tuesday.

Few people wanted to talk homers and strikeouts, but almost everyone wanted to meet Derek Jeter.

"I sort of feel a little more useful now. That is the only way to describe it."

Bernie Williams

"You go and see the firemen and all the rescue workers and they ask you for your autographs," Jeter said. "You feel like you should be asking them for their autographs. They are the heroes. It was overwhelming to get that kind of reaction."

The Yankees worked out for the second straight day in New York before flying to Chicago to restart the season Tuesday against the White Sox.

Many of the players—including Roger Clemens, Andy Pettitte, David Justice and Tino Martinez—hadn't made it back to New York, but were expected to join the team in Chicago.

Torre, who compared his visit Saturday to a trip to the U.S. soldiers in Vietnam in 1966, hopes baseball's return will help the nation's healing.

"Maybe we can help in trying to lighten the mood," he said. "We're not going to make people happy, but maybe we can give people a couple hours away from all of this."

AMERICA'S HEROES

"*You feel like you should be asking them for their autographs. They are the heroes.*"

"As long as the United States of America is determined and strong, this will not be an age of terror. This will be an age of liberty here and across the world."

—George W. Bush

Stars Pay Tribute
to Attack Victims

By David Bauder

NEW YORK (AP)—Hollywood's finest paid tribute to real live heroes during an extraordinary benefit for victims of the terrorist attacks that was hard to miss on the television dial.

The telethon was televised Friday night on more than 30 networks, including the six biggest broadcasters—ABC, CBS, NBC, Fox, UPN and the WB.

From Tom Hanks to Julia Roberts, actors made understated appeals for donations, telling stories of innocent people killed and heroic acts. They alternated short speeches with singers such as Willie Nelson and Wyclef Jean, who performed on sets decorated by hundreds of burning candles.

"We are not healers," Hanks said. "We are not protectors of this great nation. We are merely artists, entertainers, here to raise spirits and, we hope, a great deal of money."

Nelson wrapped up the two-hour benefit by leading an all-star version of "America the Beautiful" with Stevie Wonder on harmonica. He

The stars of the show were not Tom Cruise, Julia Roberts and Chris Rock, but the people whose stories they told— like John Parry, a police officer who gave his life on the day he was to file his retirement papers; Shannon Greenfield, a schoolteacher who risked her own life to carry a pupil away from one of the falling World Trade Towers; Michael Judge, a priest killed while administering last rites to a dying firefighter; and Tim Brown, another firefighter who dug through rubble in search of his friends.

"We are not healers. We are not protectors of this great nation. We are merely artists, entertainers, here to raise spirits and, we hope, a great deal of money."

followed Canadian singer Celine Dion's version of "God Bless America."

Paul Simon, wearing an "FDNY" cap, sang a version of his venerable hit, "Bridge Over Troubled Water." Mariah Carey sang "Hero" in one of her first public appearances since her breakdown.

"America: A Tribute to Heroes" was reminiscent of the Live Aid concerts for famine relief in 1985, but that wasn't available across such a wide spectrum of networks.

Within the first 15 minutes of Friday night's telethon, Bruce Springsteen, Wonder and the rock band U2 performed on stages in New York, Los Angeles and London.

"This is a prayer for our fallen brothers and sisters," Springsteen said opening the telecast, before singing one of his newer songs, "My City of Ruins."

Wonder condemned hatred in the name of religion before singing "Love's in Need of Love Today." Neil Young performed the late John Lennon hit, "Imagine." Tom Petty and the Heartbreakers played their defiant, "I Won't Back Down." Jean, dressed in stars and stripes, sang Bob Marley's "Redemption Song."

With such stars as Tom Cruise, Roberts and Jim Carrey and a two-hour limit, it was hard to fit in everybody. Meg Ryan, Jack Nicholson, Sylvester Stallone and other celebrities were relegated to the phone bank, answering contributors' calls.

A phone number, 1-866-TO-UNITE, and Web site, www.tributetoheroes.org, flashed across the screen for donations.

The special, pulled together in less than a week with artists donating their time, was telecast live without an audience and went off with barely a hitch.

Actor Will Smith appeared with the boxer he's portraying in an upcoming movie, Muhammad Ali, to remind viewers not to target all Muslims in the wake of the Sept. 11 attacks.

"I wouldn't be here representing Islam if it were terrorist," Ali said. "I think all people should know the truth, come to recognize the truth. Islam is peace."

"Frasier" star Kelsey Grammer, dressed in black and fighting for his composure, talked about John F. Kennedy. His show's executive producer, David Angell, was killed in one of the hijacked planes that crashed into the World Trade Center.

Roberts saluted people who saved lives at the Pentagon, which also was struck by a hijacked jetliner.

"Life is so precious. Please, please, let's love one another," the actress said. "Reach out to each other. Be kind to each other. Peace be with you. God is great."

When Long Island native Billy Joel sang "New York State of Mind," a New York City firefighter's hat sat on his piano.

Building on the success of last week's all-star telethon for victims of the Sept. 11 air attacks, musical performances from the show will be packaged as a benefit album to raise additional relief dollars, organizers said.

As with the telethon, 100 percent of the proceeds from sales of the benefit album will go to the relief fund, said Barbara Brogliatti, a spokeswoman for the telethon.

A Likely Hero

Investment firm Morgan Stanley was one of the largest employers in the World Trade Center, their offices spread between the 43rd and 66th floors. The overwhelming majority of their 3,700 employees escaped the devastation alive because of the bravery of one man: security chief Rick Rescorla.

Rescorla was also there at the 1993 bombing of the Trade Center and ushered many employees to safety. One Morgan Stanley employee recounted how Rescorla took matters into his own hands to take control of the crowd that day. "To get their attention, he dropped his pants," recalled Sam Fantino. Fantino was Rescorla's radio operator in Vietnam, where Rescorla was a lieutenant and platoon leader. Fantino also said that Rescorla used unconventional methods in war, too, singing to his men during tense moments to encourage them to continue fighting.

Only 15 of the Morgan Stanley employees remain unaccounted for in the aftermath of September 11. Tragically, one of them is Rick Rescorla.

Everyone who knows the robust Rescorla and his booming voice says that he was someone you'd want in charge of such a situation and is the reason that so many made it out alive.

"Rick was down toward the base trying to make sure people got down and out," according to Bob Sloss, a managing director at Morgan Stanley who last saw Rescorla around the 10th floor in the stairwell. "He was definitely there well after it had been established that the building was in trouble."

Born in Hayle, Cornwall, in England in 1939, Rescorla was a mercenary for the British Army forces in Zimbabwe and also was a police officer in Rhodesia before he came to the United States in the early 1960s and joined the Army.

Rescorla put himself through college on the G.I Bill at Oklahoma University and earned a master's degree and a law degree. He retired as a colonel in the Army Reserve and worked for the past 18 years in security management for Morgan Stanley, where he worked his way up to first vice president for security.

Rescorla's heroics in the chaotic tragedy of the World Trade Center attack surprised few.

"If anybody could get people out or do anything to help," his wife said, "it was my Rick."

Heroes Carry Woman in Wheelchair 68 Floors to Safety

Many stories of selfless acts of bravery have come to light in the aftermath of September 11. People terrified for their own safety— with no idea what had happened to the building or what to do next— stopped to lend a hand, some comfort or to literally risk their lives for another's.

Michael Benfante and John Cerqueira are two of those people who didn't listen to their own instincts for self-preservation. They paused to help a woman in a wheelchair down 68 floors to safety through smoke and confusion.

Benfante, 36, and Cerqueira, 22, work for Network Plus, a Boston-based telecommunications firm with 26 employees who had worked in Suite 8121 of the North Tower of the World Trade Center.

Branch manager Benfante's first thought was that there had been an earthquake or that perhaps a small plane had hit the building by mistake.

"I ordered everyone out of the office and down the stairs," he said. "I saw flames flickering to the side of the building, and I could feel the building swaying."

On the way down the stairs, the pair came across Tina Hansen in a wheelchair stranded at the 68th floor. They lifted her out of the wheelchair and placed her in a special handicapped escape chair and began the long descent to the bottom of the tower.

After they had placed her into a rescue vehicle, the building began to crumble, and the two were forced to run for their lives.

"We made it a few blocks when the building just exploded," Benfante said. "Everything went black. Smoke and debris were everywhere."

After taking shelter under a truck until they were able to see, the two sought shelter in a church on 13th Street.

Rescue workers drive an all-terrain vehicle past ground zero.

"We are not afraid today. Get back on the airplanes. Get back to work. Rebuild America. Together we will get through it because we are the United States of America."

—Rev. Calvin Butts

Officer Howard
Emerges as N.Y. Hero

By Deborah Hastings

NEW YORK (AP)—He was, he always insisted, just a regular guy doing a job.

He gave no thought to the box of medals awarded to him by the City of New York. George Howard knew he was lucky. Many men pass through life tolerating their jobs. Howard was blessed with loving his.

In the 1993 World Trade Center bombing, Howard rescued an elevator packed with children—on his day off. He wasn't scheduled to work Sept. 11 either. And no one asked him to. He just went. And died for it. An ordinary guy doing an extraordinary job.

Days later, Arlene Howard gave her son's most prized possession—shield number 1012 of the Port Authority Police Department—to President George W. Bush, who carries it as a reminder, he says, that his work is just beginning.

The president held up Howard's shiny silver badge during a televised speech before Congress last week.

"The American people have got to understand that when I held up that badge, I meant it. This war on terrorism is my primary focus," Bush said, announcing plans to choke channels of terrorist funding.

Mrs. Howard believes him. She also believes her 44-year-old son wouldn't have liked all this fuss.

But when Port Authority officials asked if she'd give George's shield to George W. Bush, she couldn't refuse.

"I told him not to forget everyone who went in there to save people's lives," she said.

The Howards buried George last week. His body was found by a detective who saw a gun sticking out of the ruins of the World Trade Center, destroyed in a terrorist attack two weeks ago. The gun was strapped in a holster that was strapped to George's waist. Rescue workers gingerly pulled away a piece of siding and carried him to an ambulance.

Howard had arrived just before the second tower crumbled. When it did, he was killed by the avalanche.

He leaves two sons, Robert, 13, and Christopher, 19. The elder plans to follow his father's career path. The younger isn't so sure.

"I don't know whether he realizes what happened," said his grandmother. "He's going to be lost without his daddy. I don't know how he'll cope after it's over and all these people aren't around."

George's brother, Patrick, is a New York City police officer. The job of delivering the awful news to their mother fell to him. On the day of the attacks, Patrick went to George's office at John F. Kennedy International Airport to see if his brother had checked in after getting to the site.

Officer George Howard

President Bush comforts Arlene Howard, mother of police officer George Howard who was killed during the collapse of the World Trade Center.

He didn't have to ask if George had gone there. He knew his brother. He also knew that if his brother were alive, he would have called his bosses to let them know he was on the job.

"I'm trying to be strong," said Mrs. Howard. "And Patrick is the same as me. But you have your moments and your thoughts and your days."

George Howard, a 16-year veteran of the department, was a founding member of its elite services division. He also trained firefighters in search and rescue techniques.

When he was awarded the Medal of Valor for rescuing children trapped in the 1993 Trade Center bombing, he brushed it off with humor. "That's what they pay us for," he told a reporter.

His mother was used to hearing that. "I'd say, 'Well, George, you got this medal.' And he'd say 'Yeah, mom, that's my job.'"

George wanted to be a firefighter when he graduated from high school in suburban Long Island. For some reason his mother never knew, he didn't get into the New York City department.

"So he went to the police department (of the Port Authority) and got a job that was a combination of both. He had a job as a fire instructor and he rescued people," she said.

After the president held up her son's badge on national television, Arlene Howard has been deluged with mail. The symbolism of her gesture was not lost on the American public. Law enforcement badges are never retired; they are passed on to family members as cherished symbols.

But she doesn't want it back.

"I want them all to be remembered," she said.

And as she looks through the bags of mail that have poured in from all over the country, she wonders who this "hero" is that has received such praise.

"All these people are telling me how wonderful he was and to me he just said, 'Oh, that's my job.'"

"An ordinary guy doing an extraordinary job."

Pledges Support
Education Funds

By Arlene Levinson

An education foundation pledged $3 million Monday to provide college scholarships for the spouses and children of those who perished or were disabled in the terrorist attacks.

The Families of Freedom Scholarship Fund was created by the Indianapolis-based Lumina Foundation for Education to aid undergraduate education of financially needy survivors. The scholarship is being offered in partnership with the Citizens' Scholarship Foundation of America, based in St. Peter, Minn., which will take applications and donations and manage the money.

"The devastating loss of Sept. 11 will affect thousands of families for years to come," Lumina's Edward McCabe said in a statement. "Education is a vital way to triumph over life's obstacles." To that end, Lumina is giving $2 million outright and another $1 million in matching funds to encourage individual donations. The organization also hopes to raise money from corporations and other groups.

Last week, the Marine Corps-Law Enforcement Foundation said it would give $10,000 in scholarship bonds for children whose parents were killed in the terrorist attack on the Pentagon.

Lindsey Roberts, a student at Juniata College in Huntingdon, Pa., is leading a fund-raising drive to one day provide full tuition to the child of a rescue worker killed when the World Trade Center was destroyed.

The school of medicine at Marshall University, in Huntington, W. Va., is creating a scholarship in memory of a 1995 graduate, Dr. Paul Ambrose, who died in the plane that crashed into the Pentagon.

"Education is a vital way to triumph over life's obstacles."

Victims Mourned at Pennsylvania Crash Site

By Todd Spangler

SHANKSVILLE, Pa. (AP)—Using a cluster of hay bales for a memorial, family members and friends of the victims aboard hijacked United 93 left flowers, photographs, teddy bears and other mementos.

"Today, I was lucky enough to overlook some hallowed ground for our country," said Gordon Felt, whose brother Edward died when the plane, one of four taken Sept. 11 by terrorists, crashed in a field 80 miles southeast of Pittsburgh. "It's probably the first of many visits that will bring closure."

First lady Laura Bush attended a second memorial service, held under a tent on a golf course about four miles from the Pennsylvania crash site. At each end of the tent were vials of soil from the crash site for mourners to take home.

"One of last Tuesday's victims, in his final message to his family, said that he loved them and that he would see them again," Bush told the 300 people present. "You grieve today, and the hurt will not soon go away. But that hope is real, and it's forever, just as the love you share with your loved ones is forever."

"But that hope is real, and it's forever, just as the love you share with your loved ones is forever."

Best Friends

Abe Zelmanowitz's brother Jack had one question for him: "Why are you still in there?"

Abe had called his brother after the first plane hit the World Trade Center to tell him he was all right. But Abe would not leave, despite his brother's frantic urging that he needed to get out quickly.

Why? Because his good friend, Ed Beyea, was paralyzed from the neck down, and Abe was not the type of person to leave him alone.

Abe Zelmanowitz and Ed Beyea had become best friends in life though they were very different. Abe, an Orthodox Jew, and Ed, a Christian, were in their office on the 27th floor of One WTC when terror struck.

While others around them frantically evacuated, Ed told Abe that he couldn't leave the office—the 42-year-old was struggling to breathe, and he obviously couldn't walk down the stairs. Ed was a very large man, and he didn't want to jeopardize anyone else's chance to escape by allowing anyone to try to carry him out.

Abe, 55, convinced Ed's nurse to leave them and find safety—that he would stay with Ed. A fireman was also by their side, offering to lend a hand.

The nurse made it out. The fireman, along with Abe and Ed —both computer programmers for Blue Cross/Blue Shield—did not.

Both men had called their families during the confusion and told them they were fine. That was before the building collapsed. Abe called his brother on his cell phone, "and we assumed he was on his way home," Jack's wife, Evelyn, said.

But during a second call minutes later, "He said he was still at work," she said. "He told me Ed was having breathing problems. I could hear a fireman in the background, and I was trying to convey, just go."

"But he wouldn't leave him," Jack said.

Ed had also called his mother after the crash to assure her he was fine. Abe dialed and held the phone to Ed's ear.

"'Mom, I'm all right,'" he said. "She said, 'Thank God.'" When the phone rang again, it was her son, who told her the devastating news.

The tower had just collapsed, taking Ed and his best friend with it.

Ed's sister said she is sure her brother—who overcame obstacles after a diving accident paralyzed him 20 years ago—urged his friend to leave him and save himself.

"I'm pretty sure Abe was Ed's best friend, and I know Abe was my brother's," she said. "He'd have to be, to do what he did."

New York University students attend a candlelight vigil for victims of the Trade Center attacks.

"Our nation, this generation, will lift the dark threat of violence from our people and our future. We will rally the world to this cause by our efforts, by our courage. We will not tire, we will not falter and we will not fail."
—George W. Bush

"What makes someone want to do this work?"

One of America's greatest living writers expressed his respect and esteem for the brave men and women who risked their lives to save others during the World Trade Center tragedy. Author Kurt Vonnegut Jr. reflected, "The most stirring symbol of man's humanity toward man that I can think of is a fire truck."

Few of us can imagine the horror and fear that the thousands fleeing the twin towers must have faced. It seems beyond comprehension to understand the makeup of a person who makes it his or her life's work to run toward such a disaster for one reason only: to save the life of another.

A patient recovering in a burn unit in the aftermath of the attack tried to remain positive as he described his escape and the long recovery he was facing. "But I have to live," he said, "if only to honor the lives of the rescuers who died.

"All those firefighters and police officers — we saw them going up the stairs as we were going down. . . . I really just want to say thank you to them."

As the days passed and the count of missing firefighters continued to rise, still their brothers maintained hope.

"There ain't no death toll," an exhausted firefighter working in the mountain of debris insisted, "they're just unaccounted for."

But as it became clear that no more of their fallen comrades would be found alive, members of this amazing brotherhood, along with the rest of the country, began to pay their respects and mourn the loss of these heroes. The memories and stories of the people who were willing to put their lives on the line every day resound in numerous services around New York City.

One such amazing story belongs to Capt. Timmy Stackpole.

At a small corner in the smoldering piles of debris, a hush spread over rescue workers the night of September 11 after a firefighter's body was found, silencing shovels and the din of machinery.

Bowing his head, a firefighter said quietly: "It's Capt. Timmy Stackpole."

AMERICA'S HEROES

Stackpole's incredible story of perseverance and dedication to the Fire Department had already been etched in the department's history long before September 11.

Stackpole was described as a miracle firefighter, the man who worked his way back to full duty after he was nearly killed in a Brooklyn blaze. He was the Great Irish Fair's Irishman of the Year, the Catholic "Bishop" who counseled countless firefighters.

But most of all, he was a fireman who loved fighting fires.

"We called him 'Jobs' because he was always talking about the fire job we had the day before, the week before, the year before," said his friend Lt. Gerard O'Donnell, a 37-year FDNY veteran. "He now becomes part of the lore and the history of the Fire Department."

On June 5, 1998, Stackpole rushed into a burning East New York, Brooklyn, rowhouse to search for a woman mistakenly believed to be trapped inside. The floor collapsed, plunging Stackpole, Lt. James Blackmore and Capt. Scott LaPiedra into a maelstrom of flames. Stackpole recited the Lord's Prayer aloud.

Blackmore died at the scene. LaPiedra died 29 days later. Stackpole was hospitalized at Weill Cornell Medical Center's burn unit for 66 days. His injuries would easily have qualified him for a pension, but after years of painful surgeries and skin grafts, Stackpole returned to full duty in March and was promoted to captain in September.

As firefighters and priests, friends and neighbors streamed in and out of Tara Stackpole's Brooklyn home, she found a few moments of peace sorting through the clothes her husband left heaped on the floor before he dashed to the disaster scene.

In the pocket of a pair of chino shorts, she fished out a pink neon Post-It note that her husband had scribbled on—notes from a speech he gave when he was honored as the Irishman of the Year by the FDNY's Hibernian Society.

"What makes someone want to do this work?" Stackpole had written. He went on to write that it takes a "special" kind of person to become a New York City firefighter.

Mayor Giuliani called Stackpole extraordinary. "He was in fact one of the most exceptional human beings I've ever met," said the mayor, who had visited Stackpole in the burn unit after he was critically wounded in 1998. "I fit him in the category of some of the real heroes that I have seen."

And there are so many other heroes . . . .

Like Terrence Hatton, 41, a Rockville Centre native and captain of the city Fire Department's Rescue 1 squad. A year ago, Hatton, who is now missing, led a daring and successful mission that saved 12 people trapped in a malfunctioning elevator on the 78th floor at Two World Trade Center. Hatton commanded 25 firefighters and three lieutenants as they entered the first tower shortly after it was attacked on September 11. Now, in virtually the same place,

"The most stirring symbol of man's humanity toward man that I can think of is a fire truck."

his colleagues are attempting to match Hatton's courage, hoping he can be saved.

It was the ultimate act of bravery in a long string that spanned a 21-year firefighting career. In 1995. Hatton responded with fire chief Ray Downey at the Oklahoma City bombing; a year earlier, he received the New York Fire Department's Medal of Valor as a lieutenant for rescuing a woman trapped in an Astoria diner.

And then there is the story of Manuel DelValle Jr., 32, whom police officers, firefighters and emergency medical workers gathered at the Mission Church in Roxbury to honor.

In the service, a friend described DelValle as a compassionate warrior and a hero who loved his people and his neighborhood. He was one of a relative few Puerto Ricans on the New York City Fire Department.

Fire Chief Peter Ganci joined the Fire Department 33 years ago and served in Brooklyn and the Bronx before rising through the ranks. As the chief of department, the highly decorated firefighter oversaw all uniformed personnel and the Emergency Medical Service Bureau.

He was remembered at his funeral as a selfless leader who died a hero.

In his homily, the Rev. John Delendick recalled Ganci as someone who "preferred to be one of the guys" and lead by example. He recalled being at Tuesday's disaster as a Fire Department chaplain and seeing Ganci "right in front, as he always is, and he was in control."

The priest added that "there are many images I hold in my heart of Peter Ganci": sitting in the corner at a party, telling war stories and imparting wisdom; playing in his beloved weekly game of golf and, ultimately, commanding amid Tuesday's collapse, doing the job he loved so much.

In his eulogy, friend and Acting Chief of Department Dan Nigro said, "Right from the beginning, the department was led by its five-star hero, Peter Ganci. He survived the first collapse, but instead of moving back out of harm's way, he went toward the collapse to supervise rescues.

Giuliani recalled conferring with Ganci at the command post Tuesday, then turning to leave. "I quickly said, 'God bless you,' and thought I would see him later."

"He had high goals and aspirations," New York firefighter Lt. Charles Hubbard said. "He was studying for promotion in the Fire Department. He was a natural leader. I saw him as moving up the ladder."

DelValle is still reported missing. Hubbard said he was last spotted in the towers, stopping to help a woman who had fallen.

These and the hundreds of other firefighters who made the ultimate sacrifice are the true heroes of September 11. And hundreds of their ranks have spent countless hours in a painstaking search through the rubble for their fallen brothers.

One volunteer at the scene brushed off any thanks for offering to help: "Those firefighters, the ones at ground zero for the last two weeks, they look like zombies: going on only hours of sleep and busting their butts to do whatever they can. We can never forget what those guys have done for our country. We can never forget what happened here."

A bronze statue has become a natural memorial for lost firefighters in New York City. The statue was on its way to Missouri when it was rerouted and donated to New York.

WTC Landlord
Envisions Four New Towers

By Adam Geller

NEW YORK (AP)—The operator of the World Trade Center said he is leaning toward erecting four 50-story buildings in place of the felled twin towers, as well as a memorial to people killed in last week's terrorist attack.

Larry Silverstein, the leader of a consortium that just months ago signed a 99-year lease on the complex worth $3.2 billion, said in an interview Thursday he is determined to rebuild for both emotional and economic reasons.

"The people who have inflicted this upon us are clearly out to destroy our way of life," said Silverstein, whose company lost four employees in the attack. "It would be a tragedy to allow them their victory."

Beyond making a moral statement, replacing the World Trade Center makes sense because lower Manhattan needs the office space, he said. The twin towers' 10-million square feet comprised about 10 percent of the financial district's total space and served as the area's economic anchor.

Silverstein has previously said he wanted to rebuild. But his comments Thursday marked his first discussion of limited specifics.

"I don't envision building a carbon copy of what was," the developer said.

Instead, he has been studying one set of plans drawn up and then put aside more than 30 years ago, to build four towers at the trade center site. But Silverstein said he has just begun trying to assemble a team of planners and architects to consider options.

Building a quad of 50-story buildings at heights similar to the rest of the Manhattan skyline would avoid creating a new set of terrorist targets as well as fears businesses might have of renting space 100 stories up, he said.

"In that fashion, you avoid the problems that could otherwise develop with two 110-story towers," said Silverstein, speaking in his company's midtown conference room lined with photos and drawings of various building projects, including a night view of the Trade Center, the Statue of Liberty in the foreground.

AMERICA'S HEROES

"We'll preserve as much of that wall as possible, because there are people who have expressed an interest in doing a memorial, which will involve some of that wall."

—Rudolph Giuliani

Silverstein leads a consortium, including shopping center developer Westfield America Inc., that in July signed a lease with the Port Authority of New York & New Jersey to operate the World Trade Center complex.

Silverstein said his company had already paid more than $600 million to close the deal. He said the contract with the Port Authority "might very well" include provisions binding the consortium to fulfill the terms of the lease.

"We're just getting into all the details now," he said of discussions with the Port Authority, insurance companies and other key parties. "But you know, it always was my decision to rebuild. . . . You can't rebuild on land you don't control."

Silverstein said he has received a flurry of letters and e-mail from the public since the attacks, some urging him to leave the site fallow as a memorial, but the majority encouraging him to rebuild.

To many people, the stark steel spine of one of the World Trade Center towers—bent and broken but still standing—seems an obvious starting point for a permanent memorial to those killed in the Sept. 11 attack.

Carol Willis, director of the Skyscraper Museum, believes a memorial should include a calming, quiet aspect in addition to the fragmented facade.

Other cities have used remnants of ruined buildings as powerful reminders. The deformed skeletal dome of the building at Hiroshima's ground zero was enshrined. Oklahoma City's memorial includes parts of the walls of the bombed Murrah Federal Building.

Architect John Petrarca is among those who favor incorporating the skeletal steel wall into a memorial.

"That piece of wall is haunting," he said. The remains, from the bottom of the World Trade Center, are "one of the few decorative features of that building."

"When you lose a loved

one, you gain an angel

whose name you know.

On September 11, 6,000

angels were added

to the spiritual roster."

—Oprah Winfrey

PHOTO CREDITS

I N T E R I O R
AP/Wide World Photos

J. Scott Applewhite—73 (top and bottom); Victoria Arocho—149; Ed Betz—4; Diane Bondareff—89; Andrea Booher—3, 52, 110; Roberto Borea—67, 86; Brad C. Bower—100; Brian Branch-Price—75, 79; Robert F. Bukaty—56; Stephen Chernin—21; Jim Cole—25; Jim Collins—128; Charles Dharapak—8; Alan Diaz—44, 87; Eric Draper—8 (far right), 137 (bottom); Richard Drew—97, 134; David Duprey—58, 63, 65; Ron Edmonds—8 (bottom right), 48, 64, 105; Ron Frehm—80; Terry Gilliam—37; David Gochfeld—59, 153; Bill Haber—55; Steve Helber—47, 49, 50, 83; Matt Houston—146; David Karp—8 (middle); Beth A. Keiser—26, 70, 118; Preston Keres—85, 103; Bill Kostroun—113; Charles Krupa—33, 139; Louis Lanzano—121, 122, 123; Mark Lennihan—96; Ben Margot—78 (top); Joe Marquette—51, 124; Win McNamee—138; Robert Mecea—145; Doug Mills—15, 117, 119, 150; Pablo Martinez Monsivais—109; Graham Morrison—69; Matt Moyer—27; Adam Nadel—155; William Philpott—107, 114; David Pickoff—13; Suzanne Plunkett—41, 61, 95, 99; Chad Rachman—8 (far left); Ryan Remiorz—102; Amy Sancetta—34, 115, 131; Wally Santana—30, 68; Tim Sloan—22, 57; Robert Spencer—8 (top); Tom Sperduto—31; Justin Sullivan—38; Mike Theiler—106; Gary Tramontina—23, 78 (bottom), 92, 141, 143, 158; Quyen Tran—156; Nick Ut—127; Suzanne Vlamis—12; Will Waldron—18; Ted S. Warren—45, 133; Jim Watson—29; Jim Wells—11; Kathy Willens—43, 90, 91; Jeff Zelevansky—39

Corbis

Thomas E. Franklin/Bergen Record—1; www.corbis.com—3, flag emblem